A Soldier Goes *to* Heaven

A SOLDIER GOES *to* HEAVEN

A Novel

JOHN M. ROBERTS

XULON PRESS

Xulon Press
2301 Lucien Way #415
Maitland, FL 32751
407.339.4217
www.xulonpress.com

Paperback ISBN-13: 978-1-66284-790-5
Ebook ISBN-13: 978-1-66284-791-2

PREAMBLE

The possibilities are endless.

When many people think of heaven, they think in terms of a disembodied spirit floating on a cloud thinking only happy thoughts.

The truth is that scripture tells us much about heaven and it is very much like the world we now live in.

I believe we will still be human, and that humans need a body. Bodies are physical, as can be attested by the body that Jesus returned to earth with. He ate food, conversed with others, sought out old friends, and continued old relationships. He walked the earth, again, on sandaled feet.

Spiritual does not negate the physical. Jesus, with his spiritual/ physical body, could disappear and reappear at other places. Will our bodies be like his? I believe so, although we may not have the abilities he has. Perhaps the life we live, *now*, will determine what abilities our bodies and minds will have in heaven. It bears consideration.

Scripture also speaks a lot about rewards. Heaven is a free gift of God. All we need to do is accept Jesus' blood payment for our sin. After that, we get rewards for serving him. I like to think some of those rewards will be greater abilities, greater purpose.

We will not go up to heaven. Heaven will come down to us, at least the holy city, New Jerusalem, will.

In this story, those who served Christ in this life will be reborn in the holy city. Those who did not will be reborn somewhere on our own home—earth cleansed and purified so we can live forever under the rule of a perfectly just and benevolent king. That, to me, would be heaven. Also, heaven would be a place where saved, but still very imperfect and damaged, people could mature and grow into that person they were meant to be.

We will still remember, but maybe not immediately. I see life in heaven as a life of growth, adventure, and learning.

The new earth and New Jerusalem will be populated by billions of maturing people from hundreds of civilizations and thousands of societies. From cave dwelling aborigines of the far past, through ancient Rome, Greece, China, Russia, Africa, America, etc. to modern times with modern technology and modern knowledge--they will all be there with the urge to rebuild. How many years will it take Stradivarius to make his new first violin? Or how long before the first steam driven riverboat? People will live in heaven who know how to build a cell phone. When will cell phones arrive and will they be needed? What about motorcycles and electric cars? What about the two hundred or so suppressed inventions like antigravity or the hydrogen fuel-cell? The knowledge will be there. Fortunately, Jesus will be in charge of heaven's growth, and we will be sure to use our old knowledge wisely.

That said, it is wise to keep in mind our duty in heaven is to look to Jesus for guidance to the growth of civilization and our own spiritual growth.

Why did God decide to make New Jerusalem the way He did? Scripture gives us the dimensions of the holy city: 1500 miles wide, 1500 miles long, and at least a part of it will be 1500 miles high.

If the center sits on old Jerusalem, in Israel, the north wall will cross Turkey, the west wall Greece, the south wall southern Egypt, and the east wall as far as Kuwait. I like to think the height will be gained by a great tower sitting on mile-high foundations with the garden of Eden on its ground floor surrounding the old city of Jerusalem.

In this story, the tower consists of many levels. Anyone can go to any level and live there—if they want to—if they feel spiritually comfortable enough. Whatever the true situation of our future lives in heaven, …the possibilities are endless.

Behold, I will create a new heaven and a new earth.
They will build houses and live in them; they will
plant vineyards and eat thereof. Isaiah 65

The year: 297 N. B. (New Beginning)

CHAPTER ONE

...and there was no longer any sea. Revelation 21:1

Maria Rosetta Garcia stepped carefully as she hurried up the hill to the Birthing Shrine. She smiled, glancing up the trail in thought, and stopped, frowning to pull her long skirt to reveal her bare feet. "Ouch, that's the second time this week." Her big toe seemed normal, and the pain was already fading, but, just the same, one should still be careful.

The path wound around full, green bushes and trees at the beginning of bud. The violet of new flowers already tinted upper branches.

The well-worn rocky path made one last turn as Maria paused to stare at the door of the shrine. It always stayed open-unless a new-birth had arrived. She grinned and hurried the last few feet up to the closed door, then stopped to compose herself. Fidgeting with excitement, she brushed her hands quickly down her skirt and blouse smoothing nonexistent wrinkles, and paused to take a deep breath. Perhaps she would be blessed to find a child, or bless His name, a baby. She so wanted to raise a small one. Her village had only received two this year—not much for a village this size.

She pushed the door open, propping it with a peg lying on the floor, and walked into shaded warmth. Light beams streamed through vents high up ancient stone walls. Hurrying across the vestibule, she approached the doorway of one of the rooms in the side passage and, pausing again, went to a knee and said a quick prayer. Rising to her feet, she pushed the door open and stepped inside.

A man lay on a narrow bed of woven cotton and wool.

Sighing, she reminded herself that any new birth is always cause for celebration. Patiently, she knelt down by the sleeping figure and waited.

Captain Caleb Carson, a soldier by trade and adventurer by profession, woke quickly but lay a moment with eyes closed. He knew something was wrong. He heard the quiet sibilance of wind blowing past a high window and knew he was in a small room. He lay on a comfortable cot. He could smell the wool of his blanket and hear insects outside the window and knew a person was only a few feet away trying to stay still. Opening his eyes, a slit, he turned his head enough to see a young, portly woman's smiling face two feet from his bed.

"Who the hell are you."

"Hello, sir," Maria said. "I'm Maria. And that is one word you don't want to use here."

"Hunh? Here, where is here?" the captain mumbled. "The last I knew, I was high-tailing it out of Dodge—I mean, I was evading the enemy. I must have been hit or something." He opened his eyes further and looked down at his toes. Feeling his body, he found nothing amiss.

"How long have I been unconscious?" he asked.

"I know you are confused, but everything will be good. You'll see. I'll introduce you to the mayor and the others. You will really like our village."

Ignoring the words, he asked, "What about my friends, the other guys with me. Did any of them make it?"

"Just you, for now."

Caleb sat up slowly, feeling like he had slept for a long time. Frowning at the room around him, he stared at the young woman kneeling on the stone floor.

"I'd really like to know where I am, at least."

Standing, Maria said, "It was called Savannah, Georgia. But a lot of things have changed. You'll see. You are so blessed. You've had our Lord's protection. Your angel brought you here last night."

People in these remote villages saw angels behind every tree, Caleb thought, so he ignored her comment, but knew something was very different; he had never felt so calm and rested and clear-headed. None of the usual aches, either. He felt young.

"Okay, so you say I'm in Savannah, Georgia. I've obviously been here for a while. And your doctor or medicine man or whatever knows his stuff. I feel great. So, show me around. I've been to Savannah a few times."

Maria rose to her feet and beckoned him to the door. "Follow me. I've got much to explain before you meet the others. Since I'm the one to find you, I get to do it."

He followed her out of the room and across the vestibule and frowned again at the age of the stone walls. As he stepped outside, he stood by her and stared out at the view from the top of the hill.

"That's the old South Carolina River and that's New Savannah." Maria pointed down at a large village nestled by the river.

Caleb said, "You've got something wrong. This can't be Savannah. Where's the ocean?"

Maria laughed. "Oh, it's about two-hundred miles to the east, though it's really only a lot of lakes."

"You gotta be kidding me," Caleb said, shading his eyes with a hand.

"Well, no. It's been a long, long time. You've been asleep till the time was right."

"I don't know what you're talking about," he said, looking down at her round face. "You smile a lot. Get to the punch line, okay?"

Maria tried unsuccessfully to hide her smile. "Okay, this is it. You died a long time ago. And now you're in heaven."

Maria escorted him down the trail to the outskirts of the village chatting all the way. He kept glancing down toward where the ocean was supposed to be. All he saw was thick forest and scattered fields. The village was large and at the far end old three story brick and concrete ruins jutted up from treetops. People were out and about, carrying bundles and standing around talking and laughing. By the time they were among the buildings, he and Maria were surrounded by people.

"What's your name, sir?" A boy of about seven had skipped ahead of the others and was hanging by his side staring up at him. He carried a small brown puppy in his arms.

"Caleb. What's yours?"

"Tam. I'm nine."

"Tam, give the man some space. He just got here." A tall thirtyish gentleman stepped forward and extended a hand. "Mayor Busby. Good to meet you. I see you're in good hands with Maria. She always gets up to the shrine early."

Caleb glanced around at the gathering crowd. "Mayor, it seems you have a friendly village here. I hope you don't mind, but I need to park somewhere and think this through. I could also use a glass of water."

"Of course. Maria will show you to our pub. Plenty to drink, and if you're hungry..."

At the mention of food, Caleb casually put a hand to his stomach. "That sounds good. Thanks."

Most of the curious villagers scattered back to where they came from. A few followed him and Maria down the manicured street to the center of the village where a fountain had been erected. Water bubbled up and cascaded down carved figures of animals and flowers to splash into a raised pool. As they walked by, Caleb dipped a hand into it and raised a little to his mouth, then splashed some over his face. As he dropped his hand, he noticed the back of his hand. The worst scar of his career was gone.

Caleb stared at it a moment, turning his hand to better light. He took a deep breath, shrugged, and glanced toward the mayor, "Good water."

As they approached the pub, he saw a few men sitting at outside tables kicking back clear glasses of amber liquid. Caleb thought, This might be heaven after all. A sign above the door proclaimed, 'Gene's Fine Cuisine--Thanks be to God.'

They stepped inside to cool air and the strong smell of roasted ...something. The bar had been built along the back wall, leaving a large common area. They selected a table near the entrance and sat.

Maria sat next to him and placed a hand on his arm. "I can tell you're having a hard time. You've only been here a few hours, but you'll adjust quickly."

The mayor nodded.

Tam, standing next to Caleb, stared up at him in frank curiosity. The puppy had scampered away, looking for leftovers.

Maria took Tam's hand and pulled him over to her, wrapping her arms around his thin frame. "Please pardon Tam. He's only been with us a few weeks. He's not met a newly risen before."

Caleb turned toward her and stared for a moment, digesting the phrase, 'newly risen.' Then he shook his head. "Sorry, but a few hours ago I was with my men trying to figure out a way to stay alive. It was tense, to say the least." He held up his hand to show them the back. "My scar is gone. I get it. My men are gone—have been, for who knows how long—and I'm surrounded by friendlies trying to…" He paused and stared down at the table. "My old life is gone. Probably forever. Not that I miss it much. I was getting tired anyway, but it was what I knew."

The mayor leaned forward. "And now you have all the time you want to do what you want. There's a lot to discover and a lot to learn. A man such as yourself surely understands the horrors of war, not to mention the futility. We have no more war, but that doesn't mean there is no danger. You can jump out of a tree and break a leg just as in the old life. And it will hurt, but only for a little while and it will be fine by the next morning."

The mayor continued, "You can travel if you want. A few of us old hands have walked completely around the world. It's amazing. You'll see. There is no way I could describe it well. Also…"

Tam interjected, "Mr. Willis found another ship. He's looking for volunteers."

"Right, a lot of treasure ships have been found out in the 'Lantic Basin. Interesting stuff is found, old mysteries solved," the mayor encouraged.

Maria put a hand on Caleb's arm. "Perhaps, we should let Caleb get a feel for the village. We can set him up in Wang's old place. No telling when he'll be back from his wanderings. He won't mind."

A waitress stepped from behind the bar and approached with a pad and pen. "Who's eating and who's thirsty?"

Caleb raised a finger. "Is that beer those guys outside are drinking?"

"Of course. This is a happy place," the mayor said, with a grin. "Though, you'll find you can't get more than a buzz. You have a new, improved body. It just burns off all that alcohol like, well...fast. It does give you a bit of an energy buzz, though."

"Alright, whatever beer and whatever dish you got."

"We have fish sandwiches, roasted potatoes, salad, and veggie stew," the waitress replied.

Caleb raised a nose. "Well, what's that smell? That smell's good."

"Oh, that's the potatoes. It's a favorite around here. It'll be another ten minutes."

"I'll have all of that then."

"Some for me and Tam, also," Maria said.

Two hours later, Caleb, Maria with Tam in tow, and the mayor had wandered down the main street in the direction of the river. They stood on the bank of the old South Carolina River where the docks were located before the restoration. The river no longer slowed at the bay but flowed by swiftly to continue south for another two-hundred miles to the first of many large lakes dotting the Atlantic Basin and the Caribbean.

"I remember the old town," the mayor said. Pointing at corroded concrete posts extending up from cracked pavement, he said, "I lived here most of my previous life. I'd hang out around the docks. There were lots of restaurants and coffee shops at one time. It was quite lively. Don't miss it, though. Despite the partying atmosphere, I never felt quite at peace. But I eventually came back. It's home again."

"When was that?" Caleb asked.

Mayor Busby took a deep breath. "About seventy years ago. I was rebirthed in a little town in Italy called San Marino forty years after

the final battle. The place was hardly touched by the war, considering
how devastating it was. Lived there for a hundred and twelve years,
then started my travels. Visited most of the world for fifty-or-so
years and found myself right back here. Old memories drew me back,
I suppose."

Maria said, "I've been here most of my time. I like it here, even
though I grew up in Spain and was rebirthed in restored London."

"How long ago?" Caleb asked her.

"I was rebirthed twenty years after the war. That's, ah…" she
turned toward the mayor.

"About two-hundred- sixty years, I think. We'd need to consult a
scribe to be certain," he said.

Caleb pointed at his own chest. "Are you saying I've been asleep
for three hundred years?"

"No, you weren't actually asleep the whole time. It's difficult to
describe. You were very much alive, but you don't remember it. It'll
come to you later, but you lived in a place called Paradise for a thousand or so years, then you stood before the Lord God in judgement."

The mayor gave Caleb a tense look. "I didn't remember Paradise
till fifteen years after my rebirth and another six years till I remembered standing before the Lord in judgement. Take my word for it. It
was a difficult memory. I won't try to describe it to you. Yours, when
the Lord decides to give it to you, may be quite different than mine
or Maria's."

"I don't get it," Caleb said. "Why would God hold back memories?"

Maria put an arm around Caleb's waist and hugged him. "Because,
my brother, that was the time you had to face all you have done in
your life—all the good and all the bad. Don't worry. You'll remember
at the right time. You'll be strong enough, then. And you have us to
help you through."

CHAPTER TWO

For a few peaceful days and nights, Caleb wandered through most of the village and slept outside under the stars thinking often of the difference between this and being on a mission where sleep was often hard to find and sometimes only after putting out sentries. Finding a large mimosa tree near the river one afternoon, he settled down on padded green moss to stare out at detritus of old logs and flotsam floating by toward the Atlantic Basin.

Of course, Savannah had changed. Caleb realized the river was wider here than he remembered, and the contours of the land seemed a little hillier. He tended to remember his surroundings. His life had depended on that many times in the course of his career.

An alligator sunned itself on the far bank. A small colony of storks perched in branches close by, white and noisy. Caleb was puzzled by the presence of the alligator. He'd always considered them a dangerous nuisance.

Leaning comfortably against the smooth bark of the ancient tree, his thoughts wandered back to his previous life and his childhood.

He'd always been a bit wild for his age. Always outdoors building forts and playing soldier. Up till age twelve he'd been forced to attend church, but when his dad died around that time, his mother couldn't manage him alone and finally gave up making him go.

He thought, I wonder if Mom would be surprised by my being here? And Dad?

He sat forward. "Mom and Dad? They would be here, right? Somewhere?" He stood, leaning a hand against the tree as he considered. Then, with a will, he headed back into the village to the house where Maria lived.

It was easy to find Maria's house. He knew she lived close to the trail leading up the hill to the shrine and stopped to ask a kind neighbor for directions. Her house was the one surrounded by flowers. He'd honestly never seen so many flowers of so many colors all packed into a single yard. A stone path led to a wide-open front door. The simple home reminded him of shacks he'd seen in the back hills of the Appalachians.

He stood in the doorway for a moment listening to the shuffling of dishes and humming, then knocked on the doorpost.

"Come in." He heard her answer without pause.

Reluctant to enter, he waited a moment. The shuffling stopped and she appeared at the door.

"Caleb, come in. I'll make you tea."

Caleb remained at the doorway and looked down at her. "I have a question."

"Of course. You must have many."

"This one's important."

"Go on," Maria said.

"I want to find my dad and mom."

"Of course, you do. We all do. Please come inside and sit with me. You have all the time you need. They aren't going anywhere you can't find them in good time." She waved him in.

Caleb stepped inside to a rough wood floor and low ceiling. A table sat at the edge of the one large room near an open window. A cool breeze wafted in.

Sitting, Caleb remarked, "I saw an alligator by the river..."

She waved her hand toward the window. "Aw, they're harmless--at least to us. They keep the river clean of dead fish and the like."

He sat a moment in silence, thinking.

"So, you want to find your parents," she prompted.

"Yeah. I suppose most people would. Did you?"

She nodded. "I found my mother in Spain about two years after my rebirth. We were close. I never knew my father. Had no desire to go looking."

"So, she went back to live in Spain. The same place you grew up?"

Maria nodded, again.

"Did it go well? Your meeting."

Maria stood and went to a table by an adjacent wall. She poured two cups of tea and brought them back, smiling at the memory. "She was waiting for me. Had been for about ten years. She was happy. Had lots of friends in her neighborhood. She somehow knew I was coming about five minutes before I got there. She hugged me like never before, then introduced me to her friends who were visiting. We talked a long time and I stayed with her for a couple of years. It was wonderful."

"Why did you wait so long? Two years?"

"I was a little apprehensive about what I might find, I suppose. Would she be with my father again? Would I be in the way? I needed time to think it through."

Caleb shook his head. "This doesn't sound anything like what I thought heaven would be like. We aren't supposed to worry or fret over anything. Only happy thoughts, forever. That's what I heard in Sunday School."

"Caleb." She leaned forward with a teacup in hand. "I have never experienced anything here that wasn't balanced by inner peace. I'm constantly stepping on rocks and bruising my feet. We only feel enough pain to warn us to be careful. I could always put on a pair of shoes; we have a cobbler here. I just like being barefoot."

Caleb stared at the cup in his hand, saying nothing.

She continued, "It's like this: To be human is to grow. You know, in all the ways humans grow. We like to constantly learn, experience new things. We would get so bored if there was no challenge and no risk. Our bodies are indestructible because they repair so quickly, but if you test our Lord and jump off a cliff, you will have a rough couple of days before you're free of pain again. We also have a new affinity for the pain of others as well as their happiness."

"But…" Caleb struggled for words, "if I had known this, I would have lived my life a lot different."

"As we all would." She paused a moment. "So where did your mother grow up?"

"In London, in the late nineties."

"Would that be in the 1990s?" she asked.

"Yeah."

"So, you would probably want to start there. But you should think on it for a while. Set up in Wang's place. He won't mind. He takes off for two or three years at a time. He left again about a month ago. I'll help you."

"I appreciate that for the short term, but I think I'd like to build my own place if I can find the tools and a good spot."

Maria laughed and waved her hand. "There are plenty of spots to pick. You might even want to remodel one of the old warehouses where the docks were. Still, plenty of that kind of place around here. Meanwhile, consider going out with Mr. Willis on one of his forays.

He found a container ship half-buried in mud. Should have lots of goodies still in decent shape."

Wang's place was a warehouse on the second floor of an obviously ancient brick building. It looked like a bank building, which had been extensively renovated over a lot of years. It sat in the middle of what originally was the city. It was mostly destroyed in the great war and resettled as the small village slowly grew into a small town.

When he first walked in the front door, he instantly recognized Wang for the packrat he was. The front room was full of bookshelves containing ancient books from all over the world. Most were about one form of technology or another. Another room was set aside for electronics and various mechanisms. On shelves and tables were stacked radios and radar boxes, old carburetors, and electric motors.

Caleb approached a table and was surprised he recognized the motor and gearbox of an old Tesla. He didn't see a battery pack, though. Looking around, but not touching, he paused when he heard someone at the front door.

"Hello. Anybody here?"

He retraced his way back to the front door where Maria stood with a grizzled middle-aged man in coveralls.

"Hi. What do you think of Wang's collection?" Maria asked. She hooked a thumb at the man beside her. "This is Mr. Willis. I thought you two should meet. I told him you were an outdoors type of guy and he perked right up."

Willis extended a hand. "Call me Jake. Or 'Hey You'. Whatever."

Caleb instantly liked him. "Caleb." He paused. "Maria says you found a container ship."

Jake straightened his back. "Yeah, she's a beaut. Really old, of course. No idea what's in there, but a lot of the containers are down in the mud. There might be some interesting stuff in decent shape. If she still has an intact safe, we might find out where she hailed from and what her cargo is."

"How do you get down into it?"

"Dig. Lots of digging, then presto, we find a hatch and pry it open. Usually doesn't take more than a day. We got flashlights, thanks to Wang, and a generator set up on our barge."

"Sounds good to me. When do we start?"

Jake smiled. "How about we head out right after we get something to eat. The others will be ready about then."

When Caleb saw the barge, he had second thoughts. He stood on the riverbank next to Jake, Maria being somewhere else, having sworn never to set foot on the thing. The river had cut a long section of bank away as the ocean had receded over the last three-hundred years. The river moved slowly here and Willis's helpers, Enzokule, Firash, Nickolai, Chen, Edward, Julia, and Tam stood on the deck watching for Caleb's reaction. The fifty-foot-long barge had been pulled close to the shore and tied to a tree root. A long board extended from the bank down to the wooden deck.

"Are you sure this thing will float?" Caleb asked.

"Of course, it floats. I made it myself. Used the finest 'Lantic cypress I could get my hands on. It was a labor of love."

"Alright, then. Danger hasn't dissuaded me yet. I'm in." Caleb walked down the plank and stepped onto the deck, which he was surprised to find, felt solid and unmoving save for the lap of the river current against its side.

Firash stepped forward and took Caleb's hand. "I'm the self-proclaimed navigator and steersman. These fine gentlefolk," he indicated the others, "are Enzokule, an old hand; Nickolai, our entertainment;

Chen- just arrived a few days ago; Julia, Edward, our very own Scotsman; and you've met Tam already."

Caleb nodded at the others. Chen and Edward pulled the heavy plank aboard.

The barge had been set up with a tarp providing shade for the few chairs sitting underneath. Boxes, rope, and other supplies were piled on the center of the deck. Firash and Edward used long poles to push away from the bank, then the stream pulled them out into the current. Another long pole with a paddle had been attached to the back of the barge for steering.

They settled in to watch the river's edge pass by. Heavy foliage carpeted the banks. Birds called and scattered at their passing.

Caleb sat cross-legged on the deck by a wooden box. He smiled at the arrangement. "I'm impressed. This is a stout piece of engineering." He tapped a knuckle against the deck. "She's more than a barge, I think."

Jake shrugged. "I was going to install an engine and prop, but Enzokule showed up."

Caleb glanced beside him where Enzokule, dark and serene, stared out at the flowing water. Enzokule smiled back.

Jake commented, "You're still new. There are surprises yet to come. You'll see."

It was three hours later, after having a snack and doze, that Jake nudged Caleb awake.

"What? Oh, fell asleep. We're here?"

"Almost. In a few minutes, we'll see a bit of rusty iron among the trees." Jake pointed. "There. Hard to see."

Squinting, Caleb saw a bit of barely discernable rust and a little blur color among the trees. The crew set about pushing toward the bank where Edward threw a rope expertly around the end of a broken branch. They tied off.

Jake pointed. "We're fortunate to have a little dry ground here. We already have a camp set up."

The ground was firm as they pushed the plank out and started unloading supplies. Fifty feet from the water's edge more boxes were piled. A cold fire pit greeted them. A tarp clung to the trees, tied off and spread out creating a makeshift tent.

The crew finished unloading and stood around Jake. "Alright, I'm ready to start digging. The site is on the other side of those trees. Let's grab some gear."

Caleb followed behind the others with Tam and Julia. They all carried shovels, except for Tam, who carried a coil of rope laid across his shoulders. The ground was getting soft and by the time they got to the side of the ship they were walking in an inch of mud. The long pitted and rusty side of the ship rose only ten feet out of the ground covered in vines and camouflaged by limbs and leaves. It extended in both directions out of sight into the trees.

Jake stood by the metal wall. "We'll start here. Above us is solid deck. Careful though, the deck is mostly up right but tilted enough to cause problems and there will be thin places. We've been here once already, saw enough to get the lay of the land, so-to-speak."

A rope ladder trailed down from the deck above. Edward stepped onto it and before long they all had unloaded whatever supplies they carried and had started snooping about.

The deck did have a bit of tilt, but only five degrees. It also was covered in trees, vines, and detritus fallen from above. The footing was solid, except for a place Jake and the others had roped off.

Caleb stepped close to the rope and stared down into a gaping hole at the waterline twenty feet below. It smelled brackish. Frogs jumped into the water making overlapping circles. Snakes slithered away. Caleb turned at Julia's approach. "I'm kind of surprised we still have snakes what with all the problems they caused at the beginning."

Julia put her hand on his shoulder to steady herself and leaned over the rope to look down. "I've found that the animal kingdom is mostly still here. The lower animals have their place in the master's plan. They still eat each other, but mostly they are the trash removers. We still have bacteria and the usual microscopic organisms." She leaned back and faced him. "Imagine if all these leaves never decomposed. It would be a mess, leaves high as the trees. But, anyway, I suppose the world is back the way He made it originally."

The conning tower was a hundred feet away and rose up fifty feet, the top broken and rusty. Julia turned at a sound from that direction. A red fox stepped from under a knurled root followed by four cubs.

Julia's voice rose in pitch, soft and gentle. "Hey, gorgeous. Are we invading your home?"

The fox paused a moment and looked around at the other invaders scattering around the deck, then with tail wagging, stepped gingerly over to them. Stepping away from the hole, Caleb stood still while the fox sniffed his leg and moved over to Julia. She went to a knee and rubbed the mother's red fur. The foxed keened in pleasure.

A cub went to Caleb and put both paws on a leg. He reached down and scratched behind its ear. "Hey, little guy."

"He wants you to pick him up."

"Oh, okay." Caleb raised the small cub to his chest and ran his fingers through its fur. "This guy is so darned soft."

Julia looked up at him. "Yeah, by this evening we'll have a lot of visitors."

"You mean like the Garden of Eden?" he asked.

"Something like that."

Across the deck, Edward stood by a fallen and rotted tree. He called, "Hey, I got a container here. It's still sealed as far as I can see."

A few minutes later most of the crew stood next to the container. Mud had flowed over the deck at this place and buried all but a section of an upper corner. Jake pushed his shovel in the soft ground and yanked out a rotted root. "This one should be easy. The roots have been rotted for a while. Let's find the end and try the doors. Maybe they're still sealed."

The others started shoveling. Twenty minutes later, the hole was getting big enough to test the doors.

Five red and yellow parrots had perched on branches ten feet away and hanging down to the deck. They were walking back and forth chattering at the humans. "Digging, digging. Shovel, shovel," the bigger one started chanting in a high-pitched singsong. The others soon joined in. Tam tried to pet one, but it sidled away.

"Why don't you guys come down here and help, eh?" Nicko looked up out of the hole and said to the birds.

The leader began squawking, then settled down to preening his feathers. Caleb burst out laughing, "I guess he told you, huh?"

Julia looked over at him. "Told him what? I didn't get it."

Edward, still looking out of the hole, turned his attention to Caleb." Yeah, that was some mean squawk."

"No, I mean the part about them being smarter than us," Caleb laughed.

"They said that?" Julia said.

"Well, that's what it sounded like to me."

"All I heard was indignation," Edward said.

"Alright, gang. The moment of truth," Jake called out. He stood by the closed doors with a pry bar in hand. A rusted padlock clung listlessly to the door latch. Jake tapped it lightly and it fell to the soft earth at the bottom of the hole. "That was the easy part," he chuckled. He turned to the others. "Anybody want to guess what might be in here?"

"Did you find any identification? I mean for the ship," Julia asked.

"No, not really. I'm assuming, for now, it hailed out of the far east. China, Japan, somewhere out that way. But it could be from Europe. Hard to tell unless we find a safe or a watertight box. If we could get down inside, I could look at the engines and the berths and figure it out, but they're probably underwater. Any guesses?"

"I'm guessing, ah, computer parts and maybe industrial equipment," Firash said.

"Okay, anybody else?"

"A farm tractor," Nicko said.

"Alright, here goes."

Jake handed the bar to Enzokule and stepped back.

Enzokule used the bar to loosen the handles, then grabbed one with both hands and yanked up. The bar rose easily, the door popped open a half inch and a little water flowed out.

"So much for watertight." Chen stood hopeful with his shovel in hand.

Enzokule pulled on the door, opening it wide.

"What is it?" Tam asked.

Firash leaned forward and scanned the inside. "It's called an airplane. It's a kit. You need to put it together. I used to have one— back when I was young and stupid."

"What does it do?" Tam was fascinated.

Caleb glanced down at Tam. He asked Julia quietly. "Where is Tam from?"

"When," she whispered back.

"Before airplanes?"

She took his arm and pulled him a few feet away and whispered, "You remember stories from the bible?"

"A few."

"The one about the man who carried the Lord's cross?"

"Yeah."

"'Simon of Cyrene' was his name. Tam is his son. Tam died in the confusion in Jerusalem following the Lord's rising to life. Maria told me a few days ago," she whispered, watching Tam as she spoke.

Caleb said nothing as he thought on what she said. There seemed to be no rhyme or reason to when or where people were reborn here.

Tam had jumped in the hole and entered the container. "Are we going to put it together and fly?" he asked.

Jake shrugged. "Sure, kid. But first, let's look around some more. Maybe the next one will be more interesting."

The dense jungle night was pleasantly warm. No mosquitos, no gnats. No snakes in the bedroll. They all lay around the campfire with whatever bedding they brought. Soft loamy moss covered the ground under the tree cover.

"...So, bugs just stay away. Just like that?" Caleb chuckled.

"Nice, huh?" Julia smiled and lay back.

"I spent most of my adult life in jungles and desert, most kinds of terrain. This is something new to me. I think I like it."

Chen sat down by his gear. "You might want to make sure food you're carrying is sealed, though. The mice and their friends aren't afraid of you at all. They'll come right up to you and ask for snacks. Feed one and you're feeding the whole family," he said, opening a pouch lying by his elbow. He pulled out a hunk of cheese and waved it around in the air. "Wow, cheese. Sure is yummy."

A minute later a large rat jumped from a branch and walked straight to Chen's outstretched hand, grabbed the entire chunk, and began dragging it back into the jungle.

"The only way to keep him from pestering you is to let him take it back to his family," he advised, as he leaned back and relaxed.

"I'll remember that, but I didn't bring anything to eat, so it doesn't matter in my case anyway."

"Don't worry about that. We're stocked up good. We got more on the barge, too," Jake said. He was leaning back on a backpack sipping juice and staring up at the stars through the canopy.

Enzokule, sitting quietly, said, "Jake, tell the new people how you found this boat. They'll find it interesting."

"Oh, alright." He considered for a moment, then said, "It was all the fault of those parrots."

There was laughter around the campfire.

"I had cruised past this part of the river--that is, Enzo and me--probably fifty times and never gave a thought to looking more closely in here. We're moving slow, fairly close to the bank and Enzo says, 'Jake, you hear that?' I says, 'I hear a lot of things. But nothing in particular.' He says, 'I hear someone in distress.' He pointed toward the bank. My interest was piqued. Anyway, it's never the wrong time to do the right thing. I says, 'Dang, let's pull over.' So, we pull over and tie off to that same branch right there and stomp around here for ten minutes looking for a distressed person. I'm standing right over there near the path, and I hear a voice above my head. "Mister, can you hand me that stick?' I look up to see that parrot, then at Enzo, then back at the parrot. Then, thinking 'whatever!', I bend over to pick up a little stick off the ground—evidently, the most perfect stick in the jungle--and I see a blue wall fifty feet into the trees. End of the story."

"Tell me it was the same parrot at the container," Caleb said.

"It was."

Chen laughed. "There's something strange about that bird."

Caleb nodded. "Yeah, that parrot. It seems like he's too smart, even for a parrot. And he's got a big ego, too."

They all stopped laughing.

"Why do you say that?" Julia said.

"Ah, well, I don't know. I'm the new guy around here. But he said as clear as day, 'You guys are the smart ones?' A question, just like it sounds."

"All I heard was a squawk."

"Me, too."

Julia quietly asked, "Caleb, when we were with the foxes, why did you pick up that cub?"

"Huh, you said to picked it up, so I did."

Julia leaned back laughing. "The Lord is so good. He also has a sense of humor. Caleb, I never said a thing. It was the fox; she told you to."

CHAPTER THREE

Two days later they had loaded the small two-man airplane onto the barge along with most of a container of kitchenware and charcoal grills. They also found a container with forty never used lithium batteries. Jake had pulled out a meter and checked them, but they were stone cold dead, of course.

As they pushed away from the shore the parrots lined up on a branch and watched them leave, saying nothing, just waving their heads side-to-side.

Jake settled down under the tarp with the others, except Enzokule. "Okay, Enzo, when you're ready."

Enzo sat down at the front of the barge and put his feet in the water and then, bowing his head, started singing an old spiritual about the power of baptism. His head nodded to an unheard beat and the barge began moving upriver against the flow.

"There's the answer to your earlier question," Jake said to Caleb.

Mid-day Jake pulled out his multimeter and checked the batteries. He had picked well. They all were charging nicely.

Caleb looked over his shoulder. "They have a charge, after all? Maybe the warm air is helping?"

Jake turned to him. "Have you ever heard of the 'ether?'"

"No, can't say I have."

"When I was a young man, it was a hot topic in Europe. The ether flows through everything, the whole world. It permeates everything." He pointed at the batteries. "Here, on the new earth, batteries charge from the ether. It's much stronger than before. I like to think of it as a wave of energy from the great city and the throne itself. You'll see very few engines that run on petrol. Hobbyists, maybe, but here batteries stay charged all the time unless they're inside a metal container in the ground. These little beauts weigh so little, we can put a few in the airplane and see what happens."

Caleb raised a brow. "Okay. No charger. This place is getting more interesting by the hour."

Enzo stood and joined them under the tarp. "We're good for the rest of the way."

Jake nodded. "If you get tired of powering this boat, we can do a backup with some of these batteries and a dc motor."

Enzo waved the thought away. "We're good for now. Maybe later."

When they arrived back at Savannah another boat had pulled up to the bank, a riverboat with a paddlewheel on the back. It must have arrived within the hour because wisps of steam from its smokestack still rose lazily into the air.

A few of the village folk met the scavengers at the bank and helped unload. They were excited to hear about the plane.

A short man stepped forward. "What kind of plane do you have? Can I see it?"

"Hey, Stanislav. I thought you'd be interested in this." Jake pulled aside a tarp he'd thrown over it.

"Nice," Stanislav bent and looked under and around the airplane kit. "Looks to be light enough for two or three guys to carry. If you want, we can take it to my garage and put it together there. We should throw away that little petrol motor, though. I have a nice little ac motor I pulled out of a run-about. It might have enough power to get this off the ground with three or four of your batteries."

"Good enough for us but talk with Firash. I think he will want to take it up first."

"Sure, I don't like flying them anyway, I like the tinkering," Stanislav agreed as he pulled the rest of the tarp off the little two-seater.

As they unloaded, Caleb wondered about the other boat at the dock. He still thought about heading to England to look for his parents. The paddlewheel surprised him. He felt like his mind was being pulled back and forth. Jake, just eight hours back, said that batteries were the way to go, but now some guy shows up on a boat with a steam engine. He shook his head and, frowning, continued to help unload.

When they arrived back in the village a party seemed to be in progress. Someone had set up tables outside around the fountain in the center of the village and food and drink were being served. An obviously homemade guitar made occasional noise as a young man tuned it. A few other instruments lay on a table where the village musicians had placed them while they ate. A short, portly man who reminded Caleb of Benjamin Franklin mingled with the crowd. They picked a table and sat.

"Want to know who that is?"

Caleb turned to face Julia, who had just walked up. "I'm curious. He seems to be popular."

"He's John Newton, from around 1750. I hear he's been most of the way around the world on that steamer, plying the rivers and lakes. He's part of the river culture."

"The name sounds familiar. Did he invent something?"

"He was a preacher on the old earth. Wrote some songs which became very popular," Julia said.

"How did you find that out? Did he tell you?"

"No, I'm from that time and I'd heard of him. Some of his songs were in my church hymnal."

"Really? The name is starting to really feel familiar. Name a song."

"How about the song, 'Amazing Grace'? You've heard that one, right?"

"He's *that* John Newton?"

"Yeah."

Caleb, watching the preparations, said, "Most of the time I was so bored in church. Wanted to be outside doing something. But yeah, I remember that song…'that saved a wretch like me.' My mother used to sing it."

"Did you know at one time, before Our Lord saved him, he captained a slave ship?"

As Caleb thought about what Julia had just said, Enzo, Edward, and Chen ambled over and heard the topic of conversation.

"Small world, huh?" Enzo said.

"Hey guys," Julia greeted them.

"I was a slave, then a slaver a few generations after him," Enzo confided.

Caleb's eyes widened. "Really?"

"Yes, and even I'd heard of John Newton. His story helped bring me around to the truth. I was a wretch, too," Enzo said. "Now I'm here. Amazing."

"Our Lord is full of mercy. It is true," Chen murmured from down the table.

"Not to change the subject, but this looks like the party is starting." Caleb pointed at the tables, the food, and newly arriving villagers.

"Oh yeah, any excuse to socialize," Firash said.

The mayor approached with Maria, who held a fluffy gray cat in her arms.

"Nice hunt, men and lady." the mayor said. He pretended to doff a hat for Julia's benefit. "The kitchenware is presently coming in handy. Our cooks like the new pots."

"Thank Jake. He found that container."

"Anyway," the mayor continued, "I'm going to give a speech—a short one—and while we eat, we're going to hear about your scavenger hunt... and other things out of my control, which may occur." He winked.

They had claimed a table by the fountain when they saw others settling in. The mayor stood on the stone rim of the fountain and waved his arms for everyone's attention. "As you know, our own Jake Willis, with his usual panache and sleuthiness, discovered another previously sunken ship. With the help of a parrot—I've heard."

Laughter spread around the gathering.

"Our generous cooks have offered to bring us our food so we can give Captain Jake of the river barge 'Lucky Find' our full attention."

He stepped down and took his seat at a table. Jake ambled over to the fountain and slowly stepped up on the rim. As he walked around the fountain, he told a highly embellished version of the parrot story, then told of their finds. "And so, my dear friends, if you want to know more of what's out there, you'll need to bring your own shovel. And in case you think I may have exaggerated, I personally guarantee at least a full sixty percent of what I said is true."

As the laughter died down Jake joined them at their table and tucked into a plate set aside by Julia.

"Nicely done," Enzo said, "though I would have given you at least seventy percent."

"That's because you are such a generous man," Firash said. "You're always making us look good."

"Rightly so," Jake said absently as he noticed the villagers begin to whisper among themselves.

A tall, thin, gray-haired man entered the gathering, working his way through the crowd, and headed toward the fountain.

Caleb nudged Julia, "Who's that?"

She whispered back, "I don't know, but I was expecting a few words from Captain Newton."

Mayor Busby hastily stood and announced, "A few words from Messenger Annas."

The villagers began to speak in hushed whispers. "A messenger here. It's been years."

"Hush, he's about to speak."

The Messenger stopped at the fountain and turned in a circle to see everyone. He held up his hands "Blessings from Our Lord and his children in the holy city. I am blessed to be among you. Forgive my cryptic entry into your village. I enjoy traveling on the river and Captain Newton generously offered to bring me to your beautiful village.

"Although you are living far from the holy city, you are as much His children as His only begotten son. I am tasked to deliver a message—a summons—if you will. One of you is called to the holy city. All are welcome to come, but, at this time, only one is called.

"It is not often I get the opportunity to speak to those in the far-flung corners of our Lord's kingdom. It pleases me to see you so healthy in the spirit and growing in grace. If I stay long in this fine place I may decide to live here and neglect my duties, so I will begin."

He raised his hands into the air. His face and hands began to glow. "The mighty God, even the Lord, has spoken and has called the earth from the rising of the sun to the going down thereof. The Lord has called to loose the bonds of injustice and set the prisoner free. Let the called consider his way. To respond or to turn away—there will be no penalty. Let Caleb Carson journey to the holy city, New Jerusalem. You have been called. May God be with you. Amen."

The Messenger's visage flashed, and with a sparkle of stars, he vanished.

Caleb sat still, not quite digesting that the messenger just said his name. Julia turned toward him, brows raised, mouth open. The others around the table slowly stood and turned toward him. The villagers jumped from their chairs and began to cheer.

Caleb put a hand on Julia's shoulder. "Julia, what just happened?"

"I've only heard of three callings during my life here, in eighty-three years. You have been called. You will need to decide what to do. This is an honor beyond words." Tears ran down her cheeks and she smiled as she wiped them away.

"Wow, brother. I've never witnessed a calling. It was awesome. You saw how he vanished and left those sparkly things behind." Chen waved his hands around in excitement.

The villagers crowded around Caleb's table and offered their blessings and well-wishes.

Caleb sat still, confused and nervous. He nodded his head, speechless. This was so much out of the blue. He could never have imagined it--not for him. He was tempted to consider that the messenger had made a mistake, then squashed the idea—it was ridiculous. The vanishing at the end sealed the message's legitimacy, for sure.

Later, after the crowd dispersed and they retired to the pub where it was quiet, Captain Newton joined them.

Jake saw him approach and pulled another chair close. "Good to see you again, Captain Newton. Have a seat."

"Thanks, I'll only be a moment. I just wanted to say I'll stay docked here at Savannah till you announce your intentions. I'll give you a ride as far as I can on the 'Mercy'. Let me know when you've decided." He nodded to the others at the table. "Sorry, I have preparations to make. We can talk later." He got up and left the still shocked friends.

It was almost sunup before Caleb managed to get a few hours of sleep. Jake, Julia, and Chen knocked on the door to his borrowed flat and stepped inside. Caleb was sitting up on the couch, groggy and concerned.

Jake plopped down by him. "Hey, buddy, don't look so worried."

"I've got reason to be worried. That was an angel, wasn't it?"

Jake nodded.

Caleb continued, "I've been thinking about what he said. You know I was a captain in the army. I had two hundred infantry under me. That's all gone. Been gone a long time, evidently. He said something about justice and setting prisoners free. What am I supposed to do? This is heaven or at least the new earth. I thought war was all done with. And after the way he vanished, what level of warfare could it be?"

Jake shrugged. "My friend, there are different kinds of war. But maybe it has nothing to do with your career in the distant past. Maybe it's something entirely different. It would be a good idea to find out. Don't you think?"

Julia sat down on the other side of him. "We would like to encourage you to go, but it's your decision. I, myself, am very curious. I've often wondered why more people don't make the journey."

Chen said, "The angel said anyone is welcome to go there."

"Have you guys been?" Caleb asked.

They all shook their heads "no."

"Scared? Uncomfortable? Concerned that the people living there will be so much better that you'll feel small and, and…sinful?" Caleb said.

Julia nodded. "Yeah, pretty much." She lowered her head as tears began trickling down her cheek. Her voice wavered. "I am... not the woman you may think of me as. We all, here, know enough to give each other the benefit of the doubt, but I can say, I have been forgiven much more than you might suspect." Her voice steadied. "I am forgiven. And I have forgiven myself, but just the same, I know the decisions I made in my past life were my own--not imposed on me. I'm responsible for them and I will always love my Lord Jesus for putting them paid. I'm trusting you feel the same."

Jake nodded with lowered head, staring at the floor. "I was a sergeant major in Her Majesty's Royal Fusiliers. 'Musket and ball. Bayonet and Blood' was our battle call. Almost twenty years of death and misery before the futility of it all drove me to my knees before the church altar. I gave it all up in that moment, but a life-time of misery lay behind me." He looked at his three companions. "I knew at that moment I was forgiven, and I would someday be in a place like this."

The living room was quiet for a moment. The air was cool on the second floor. A breeze blew through glassless window frames.

Chen, leaning against the wall, coughed, and stirred. "All my adult life I served as Samurai. I died a Samurai impaled on another man's blade. My enemies vanished in the morning mist. My death was a slow one, and in the last hour of my life, I remembered, as a child, the kind words of a missionary. Now I am here. That, my friends, is forgiveness. It seems we have a love in common."

"Yes," Julia said. "We do." She took Caleb's hand. "I will count it a blessing if you will allow me to accompany you--the one called of the Lord."

Jake put a hand on Caleb's shoulder. "Same here, friend.

Chen gave a half-bow. "It would be my honor."

Caleb took a deep breath and let it out noisily. "Well, I never really considered turning down God. I'm scared, but still curious as hel…ah, very curious. Friends would be welcome."

Jake jumped up. "Okay, then it's time to make some plans. We got packing to do and a long journey to make. I happen to have met a man who has been to the gates of that great city and told the tale. I can tell you this: it may not be easy, but it will be worth it all."

CHAPTER FOUR

Caleb used the next day to prepare himself for the long journey. First, he went to Maria's house and spent time with her, then found his favorite tree by the riverbank, plopped down, and stared out at the dark water passing by. It never really occurred to him to pray. He'd be meeting Jesus, eventually. Maybe, by that time, he would have thought of something to say. After an hour or so, his spirit settled down and he headed for the docks.

"Where have you been? We were getting concerned," Julia said.

"I needed time alone. I hung out with Maria for a while. I was going to say bye to Tam, but I couldn't find him."

Chen interrupted. "We have too many supplies. What do you think?" He pointed at the two large piles lying on the boat deck.

Caleb glanced at them. "That'd keep a platoon going for a month. I suppose we need to talk to Captain Newton and find out how far he can take us on this boat. "

Julia kicked the pile by her foot. "What if we get to the point where we have to carry all this on our backs?"

Chen stared down at the pile. "I agree. All we need to carry is three days food for each of us and a few tools to gather food. A good water bag each and maybe we each can carry a battery to use for light or whatever."

Caleb, accustomed to command, announced, "Sounds right to me. Whatever we don't use while on the boat we'll give away and keep just enough to move fast. I hate a slow march."

"I'll need to find some good boots while we travel. These light shoes won't last long." Julia lifted a foot and displayed her cloth foot wraps.

They turned at the sound of footsteps on the gangway. Jake ambled up and stopped at the pile.

"Looks like plenty." He turned to Caleb. "There will be lots of places to resupply at first. Later, maybe not so much. We'll just need to see what happens."

"Doesn't anybody have a map?" Caleb asked.

Jake shrugged. "I never needed one. It's not like I've been in a hurry for the last hundred fifty years. I always figured I'd get there when I get there."

Caleb frowned a little. "It just feels odd not having this all planned out, you know, like a military patrol or long-range recon. I'll get used to it. What else can I do?"

Jake slapped him on the shoulder. "That's the attitude I like. It'll all work out great. You'll see."

A young man approached, barefoot, with soot-stained white shirt and pants. He wiped his hands with a dirty cloth. "Mr. Carson, sir," he said to Caleb, "Captain Newton wishes to know if you and yours are all aboard?"

Caleb turned to his friends. They nodded.

"Yes, we're ready to move. Tell the captain I'd like to ask about his route when he gets free time."

The young man flipped a sloppy salute and rushed away. A few minutes later, a whistle sounded, a puff of smoke belched from the single smokestack and a long hiss announced imminent departure. The paddle stirred and began to spin ponderously. They watched as the bank slowly receded.

A few minutes later, the same young man rushed back. "Sir, the captain wishes to see you. He says it's urgent."

Caleb, Julia, and Jake followed him by taking outside stairs to the hurricane deck, where the captain stood with a hand on Tam's shoulder.

Caleb stopped at the top of the stairs. "Tam, what are you doing here? I looked all over for you."

Tears begin falling down the boy's face. He struggled for words.

"Easy, Captain Carson. The boy's been through a difficult time. We've been talking. You need to hear what he has to say." Captain Newton nudged Tam. "Go ahead, Tam. Tell him."

Tam composed himself. "Is it true that Jesus is alive?"

"Yeah, that's what this is all about. I've got to go see him about something."

"But I saw him die," he whimpered. Then stronger—"He died!" Tam yelled. "And everybody was crying. My dad was crying. All our friends were crying."

Caleb went to a knee. He recognized shock when he saw it. From Tam's perspective, he was only a few weeks from witnessing public, state-sanctioned murder. The fear, the blood, the animal behavior by the Roman soldiers, and emotional suffering of those watching—it all had come to this moment.

Caleb said quietly, "They all say he's alive. They say he rose right out of his grave and is now king of the world. He's made everything right. Everything is okay now."

Tam lifted his chin, wiping tears from his eyes. "I have to see him. I need to see him."

Quietly, Captain Newton said, "Well, what will it be?"

Caleb put a hand on Tam's shoulder, pulled him in tight, and hugged him like a father, then let him go. As he released him, he asked, "Tam, how would you like to go to New Jerusalem where King Jesus commands the whole world?"

Sitting on the soft loam by the crude wooden dock, Maria watched as the paddle wheel drifted downriver till it disappeared around a bend. A sadness overcame her, thinking of how she would miss Tam. He so needed a good mom to watch over him. She sighed and stood, turning back toward the village she had lived in so long and the people who lived here she had come to know and love.

When she got back home, she walked past the flower garden filling her front yard, hardly noticing the fragrance and beauty. Her cabin seemed larger now, almost empty. She sat by a chair near the front door and, as the hours passed, watched the honey bees flit among the flowers and birds argue as they hopped around on her picket fence.

Late in the afternoon, Mayor Busby and Enzokule stopped by.

"Maria, we brought you something to eat." The mayor produced a basket as he entered the cabin and opened it with a flourish, handing out freshly baked bread, white cheese, and fruit.

"Hey, mayor," Maria responded with little enthusiasm.

The two men pulled up chairs and sat so they all could see the garden.

Enzokule said, "I tried planting one of those petunias you gave me. I think it doesn't like my soil. It's rather scrawny. Maybe you can come by and look at it for me."

"Sure, later."

The mayor sat in silence for a few minutes and watched her. "Tam is in good hands with those guys. And Julia will keep them all straight. You know that, right?"

"Yeah, I know. I just miss him. He was so full of energy and he…I guess he gave me something to do besides gardening."

"But you're so good at gardening," Enzokule said.

"That's not the same." Maria frowned at him.

The mayor nodded agreement. "Anyway, Doris and Janey said they won't be able to go to the shrine for a few days. They were wondering if you would take their turns."

Maria shrugged. "I guess so. Maybe for a few days. I was thinking about quitting for a while, letting others do it."

"I understand, but if you will commit to, say, three weeks, I'd sure appreciate it. Take a load off me, you know."

Maria shrugged. "Okay."

The three old friends sat together for a while longer, the men trying to draw Maria's mind to other things. The mayor knew what the problem was but didn't want to come right out and say it. Maria had a strong mothering instinct and what she needed was another new-birthed to show around the village.

They left after Maria agreed, giving them a weak, noncommittal smile. The day wore on and Maria retired to her bed and, after a spell on her knees, fell asleep.

It was still dark outside when she rose and prepared for the day. She lit a kerosene lamp and set it by the door, then put her shoes on since she would be walking in the dark. She planned on getting a good start on the day. She'd check out the shrine, then go over to Enzo's home and figure out what was wrong with his petunias. She decided last night what she needed was a change. Maybe she'd go foraging in the forest with the other ladies for spices and herbs.

Picking up the lamp, she left the house and headed for the shrine.

The sun was shining through the trees by the time she reached the shrine. The door was open, so she slowed as she approached, knowing an open door indicated no new births had arrived.

She entered slowly and looked around.

"Maria."

She whirled around. A man in a white robe sat on a chair against the far wall with legs crossed and fingers folded in his lap. "Good morning, Maria."

"Good morning, sir," Maria said. "I'm sorry, but you startled me."

"My apologies, Maria. I am here to tell you your prayers have been answered."

Maria's mind felt numb. Prayer--which prayer? She had prayed for a lot of things.

She started to ask which prayer when the man disappeared in flurry sparkles.

"Oh my."

This was the first time she had ever had a personal visit from one of the Lord's messengers.

Bewildered, she started down the hallway. The first three doors were open, but she scanned the rooms to make sure. The last door was closed. Forgetting to say a prayer first, as was her usual routine, she opened it and walked inside to find four babies, naked and asleep. Two boys and two girls, lying next to each other holding the hand of the one next to them.

Maria stopped and stared. Four babies--Four babies! she thought, slapping a hand over her mouth. She ran to them, carefully pulled a blanket over them, and stepped back in amazement. Four babies! Panic began to set in. How would she get four babies down to the village? How would she carry them? How would she feed them? How? She needed to go back down and get the other women, but could she do so before they woke up alone and afraid?

She silently left the room and went back to the vestibule. The messenger was still gone. No help there. She ran outside and looked around. Maybe she could make a pallet and put a pole in it or make a backpack out of blankets.

She'd need to chance going back to the village and hoped the babies stayed asleep. Going back to the room, she looked inside to see they were still asleep, then carefully left the shrine and ran back down the hill, glad she had put on her shoes. Halfway to the village, she met two women coming up. It was Doris and Janey.

Doris and Janey waved when they saw her coming down the path toward them in a rush, waving her arms in the air.

Maria stopped, panting hard. "What are you two doing here? Never mind. Come with me. Hurry".

"What's going on? What's the rush?" Janey asked.

Maria turned her head without stopping. "Babies."

"Babies? Two of them?" Doris stopped in her tracks.

"No. Lots of babies." Maria, in a rush, fumbled for words and pulled Doris by the arm. By the time they arrived at the shrine, Doris and Janey knew the score and were in a rush too.

They hurried to the backroom to find the babies lying awake on their backs looking around the room, still holding hands.

"Oh, my Lord," Doris said and rushed over to the days old, infants. "Look at them," she cooed. "They're so precious. Let's find some blankets. We need to make diapers."

"All in good time," Maria said. "Let's get them down to the village. It's too cool up here. We can set them up in my place, if you girls don't mind, and figure out what to do with them later."

They all agreed and within a few minutes had the infants wrapped up and snug, Janey and Doris carrying one each and Maria carrying two. They were more than careful with their precious cargo while walking down the path. When they got to Maria's home, they immediately lit a fire in the hearth to warm up the single room cabin and put the kettle on for tea.

An hour later, Maria sat at the kitchen table with tea in hand. Janey and Doris sat across from her. The babies were all asleep. All was well.

After a moment of silent decompression, Doris asked the big question. "How do we feed them? None of us are making milk."

"Let's get word around the village. Maybe someone is. Maybe that's the way we find out who the Lord wants them to go to."

"Good idea," Janey said, taking a quick gulp of hot tea. "I'll go now. They could wake up anytime now, hungry and loud."

"Me, too." Doris put her cup down. "Thanks for the tea. We'll be back in a while."

A few minutes later Maria sat alone, marveling that in the next room four beautiful infants slept soundly. She knew the Lord had saved them from whatever life they would have had so they could grow up here. Maybe they died in the womb or, she shuddered, murdered before they even had a chance. Well, here they are and here they will live in this village under Maria's watchful eyes, and Janey, and Doris and the other good women of this place as well. The Lord would provide someone to feed them, and they would have a good, healthy life understanding godly love and godly truth.

A few hours later, Janey returned with Gladys and Martha, old friends, confused and excited.

Maria met them at the door. "I didn't know you two were making milk?"

Martha stepped forward. "We didn't either, till this morning. I feel like I'm going to burst. Let me see the babies."

As Maria showed them over to the makeshift cribs, she unconsciously put her hand to her chest. It felt a little sore.

A few minutes later, Doris arrived with Lisa Holloway who, she had found shopping at the veggie stand. "Hey, we got another one."

They walked into the room to see Martha and Gladys holding a baby each and smiling in relief.

Doris asked Maria. "Why are you rubbing your chest?"

Maria lowered her eyes to stare at her hand as tears of joy trickled down her face. God has chosen.

CHAPTER FIVE

The riverbank passed by slowly over the next few days and nights. Dark water swirled in eddies as the boat passed by, sending ripples that faded as they reached the green covered banks. The landscape changed from one hour to the next. One mile it would be lush jungle, then rounding a bend in the river they would be presented with open fields of high grass and sometimes a dwelling trailing smoke in the air from a lone chimney. Captain Newton said there was a lot of open space in the Atlantic Basin still to be explored. Some of the lower areas were still a bit salty. There were plenty of fish, though, if one cared to try to catch them.

Rivers connected the thousands of lakes resulting from the draining of the oceans. Since the defeat of the evil one in the great war almost three hundred years ago, the Atlantic Ocean, like all the other oceans, had been reduced to lakes and bogs, salt and fresh, jungle and flat lowland tundra.

So much had changed, but, as Caleb began to suspect, not nearly as much as he thought there would be. People were still people. They still thought like people. It seemed to him the only really important change was the world's leadership. The messenger talked about justice and freedom. Caleb liked that. The devil and his army were gone forever.

He realized in that moment he had not heard, even once, someone say, "That's not allowed," except for cursing, but why would someone want to curse? It now seemed so crass and disrespectful.

Caleb realized, then, he had already changed in at least that small way. He wondered how much this journey would take from him and how much it would give.

The place he'd claimed for the last three days gave him a fine view of the river and both banks. He'd pulled a chair close to the rail and propped his feet up. The others had been giving him space. They knew he had a lot of thinking to do.

He heard a scuffle behind him and knew Tam was approaching. Tam practically ran up the stairs and grabbed Caleb's chair to stop his energetic charge. He'd changed back into the feisty, noisy kid they knew him to be when he realized, fully, this was the heaven he'd been taught about in the temple and his family was somewhere here too.

"Slow down, Tam, or you might launch yourself right into the river," Caleb said, grabbing Tam's shirt.

Tam gushed, "Julia said supper is ready."

"Okay, I'm coming down. Tell her I'll be right there."

Tam scampered back down the stairs without breaking a leg and Caleb followed. He smelled the broiled fish and garlic from the top of the steps. Julia had joined the boat's cook and they had whipped up a feast from a giant river trout Jake had pulled in not an hour before.

"I'm more than glad we still get to eat fish. But I still miss beef." Caleb waved away Chen's encroaching remark. "I remember the mayor saying I won't crave beef after meeting one of heaven's cows--or pigs and goats for that matter. They're way smarter than they used to be."

Jake stuffed his mouth with another bite. "I figured this fish was dumber than a sack of rocks after taking that sorry piece of bait. I was kinda surprised. We can eat scaled fish just fine. But bottom feeders taste like garbage and the dolphins will ask you about the meaning of life."

Chen sat on the bench next to Jake. "I met a dolphin years ago. Turns out she'd lived from even before the time of the great millennium. She witnessed the devil's fall from the sidelines, knew the whole history of what happened after New Jerusalem came down and the oceans started drying up."

"Didn't she have a problem with her whole world shrinking?" Julia asked.

"Naw, she switched to freshwater. Said it was no problem." Chen stopped eating for a moment. "I guess she talked with a lot of sailors and fishermen."

"What's this stuffing made of?" Caleb asked.

"Ground corn, onions, salt, olive oil, and a bit of my secret ingredient," the boat's cook replied from the end of the table.

"Good stuff," Jake said.

"Thanks."

Changing the subject, Captain Newton said, "We'll be stopping off at a town tomorrow morning to get supplies and stretch our legs. We'll spend the day and night there."

"What's the name of the town?"

"New Havana."

"Cuba?" Caleb asked.

"Used to be," Captain Newton said. "The ruins of the old town is about three miles away up on the plateau. You can go up there and see it."

"There are a lot of ruins around Havana," Jake said.

Captain Newton lifted a hand. "Let's leave it as a surprise for Caleb. I want to see his face when we get there."

That night Caleb dreamed about his old life and the last time he and his men made contact with the enemy. In the dream, he had just given orders to stop their forward advance and retreat back the way they'd come when the first mortar fell. They were caught by surprise.

Caleb woke with a start and for the rest of the night sat on the top deck watching the dark water pass by and thought about his men and what became of them—how many survived and how many died the same time he did. He realized he'd completely forgotten his usual morning ritual when back at the base. He hadn't spent any time keeping in shape and determined to get some running in the first chance he got.

When the morning sun came into view above the trees Caleb opened his eyes and realized he'd fallen asleep. He felt refreshed enough and wondered what the surprise was Captain Newton referred to yesterday until they passed a stand of trees on the bank and the first pyramid came into view.

"What do you think?" Captain Newton had paused at the top of the stairs and waited.

Caleb turned in his chair. "Where in the world did those come from?"

The captain came up on the deck and took a chair by Caleb." Been there from before the flood, covered up all that time with a hundred feet of water above the tip of the highest pyramid."

"But that's got to be at least as big as the one in Egypt."

"A little bigger. And intact, even with the gold cap on top. Nobody cares about that anymore. There are four pyramids and a lot of other structures related to energy production."

Caleb glanced over to the captain. "You confused me on that last thing you said. What energy production?"

"That's what the pyramids were all about. They produced electricity from the negative ground and positive atmosphere. All the ancient pyramids sat on energy streams running through the earth. And most, like this one, were located near large rivers."

"I did not know that," Caleb said, amazed.

"They were starting to figure it out around the time you lived. Was it late two thousand?"

"Twenty-twenty-four," Caleb said.

"In my time—the early eighteen-hundreds—there was lots of interest, and a lot was being learned, but it was shut down by the archeological societies. But by the time the thinking machines were being used for people to communicate with, it was difficult to suppress."

"We called it the internet."

"Yeah, that's it."

"I've got to check one of those out," Caleb said, staring at the pyramid through the trees.

They docked an hour later. Julia had promised to take Tam into the town and keep an eye on him while Jake went to look up an old friend. That left Caleb and Chen at loose ends.

"What are you going to do?" Caleb asked.

"I think I'll check out the food stalls and wander around. You?"

"I'm going for a run, stretch my legs."

Chen looked at him askance. "If that's what you want. We'll be here all day and night. See you later." Chen walked away, leaving Caleb standing alone by the rail.

Ten minutes later Caleb walked down the ramp to the dock dressed in long pants, boots and had a fifty pound pack strapped to his back. He had been thinking about getting in shape and his way was to go full steam ahead.

He adjusted the straps on his shoulders and, sighting the largest pyramid over the buildings and trees, began jogging in that direction.

It felt good to do this familiar thing, Caleb thought as he jogged past curious onlookers. He settled into the familiar rhythm of a routine he'd done every day for the last fifteen years. Soon he'd reached the edge of town. Not the slightest winded, he continued down a well-worn dirt road that led eventually up a hill into the trees. He knew from personal experience what it was like to hit that place in a long hike where it seemed he'd not be able to take another step. They called it "the wall" and he'd always been able to hit it and push past for a short while. He expected to hit the wall by the time he reached the tree line, but it didn't come. The pack was getting uncomfortable as expected and he'd probably have a few bruises and scrape marks from the straps. That was expected also.

Reaching the top of the hill, he saw the same pyramid up close. Not pausing, he gave it a quick survey as he ran along the crest of a ridge even with the midsection of the huge structure, then seeing the Old Havana plateau in the distance, turned toward it and closing his mind to everything except getting there, he pushed himself to his limit.

A mile fell behind, then another, and another. Caleb sought the wall, but it was still far away. He reached Old Havana. With an effort he pushed out of his fast jog into a full run, then a sprint. The miles fell behind. He ran down the abandoned main street of Old Havana and past the ruins onto another dirt road leading south. The sun rose high into the sky. Caleb's legs blurred, his feet flashed, and dust rose in his passing. Finally, approaching the foothills of the mountains, he slowed, then came to a staggering halt. He stood in the road and bent with his hands on his knees for a moment, then straightening, walked a circle in the road to cool down.

He felt good. Exhilarated. He breathed deep. His lungs felt strong. The wall never came. Nothing Caleb had experienced till this moment in this new world proved to him more than this: the body he now had was not the same as the old one.

Turning toward New Havana and the river, he started walking, and having proven himself, he picked up the pace to a fast jog and headed back.

When he returned, the others were still in town. He went to the bunk he'd slept in and changed, then went up to the top deck where the captain sat next to the chair Caleb had been using.

Captain Newton sat facing the town. Without turning around, he said, "I watched you jogging away with that pack on your back and wondered if you'd return."

Caleb paused with a hand on his chair. "Sorry. I didn't think what that would look like." He sat.

"Did you find what you were looking for?" the ship captain asked.

"No, and yes, I think. "

The captain waited.

Caleb said, "I was looking for a familiar feeling. It had been my habit to jog five miles away from the base and back every morning at sunup. I always came back winded and feeling fresh, but I also was reminded every morning of my limits. As I got older, the miles got harder.

I just now ran all the way to the mountains, but never felt really exhausted. I never got close to my limit. It's kind of scary. What am I capable of now?"

The captain turned to him. "Past the old ruins, on that old dirt road?"

"Yeah."

The captain pulled out a pocket watch. "Those mountains are about forty miles from here. And you've been gone about six hours. That would put your average there and back at thirteen miles per hour."

"Are you sure? It didn't seem like it."

"I've been out there in recent memory. The mountain didn't move, as far as I know, so yeah, I'm sure."

"Then I must have done fifteen miles per hour some of the time. That's amazing." Caleb chuckled nervously. "I suppose I was also looking for confirmation, a way to cement me into this reality. I think that did it. I'm convinced—I'll believe anything you guys say now."

"Good, because it is going to get more fantastic, but all in a good way." The captain stood and put a hand on Caleb's shoulder. "How about we go into town? There's a good beer I'd like you to try. It's my favorite."

Caleb stood. "Lead the way."

A large crowd had gathered outside the café and bar. Tables were arranged haphazardly, taking up part of the narrow street. The smell of grilled something wafted out from under the roof overhang to assail the senses. Captain Newton and Caleb waded through the crowd. Many patrons smiled and slapped the ship captain's shoulder. The atmosphere was casual and kind. Occasionally a voice rose, but it was laughter. An entertainer stood on a chair by the door and told a story. Many laughed, some groaned.

Caleb felt at home and welcome. They passed through the door into the dim and smoky interior to the sizzle of frying fish, the scent of baking buttered potatoes, garlic, and simmering greens and onions. Caleb's appetite rose.

"I didn't know I was hungry till now. Now I'm famished."

"You did just run eighty miles. I'd say you're ready to eat."

A waiter approached. "Welcome, Captain. Table or bar?"

"We'll take a table, please," Captain Newton replied.

They followed the waiter to the side of the room where they were seated by a window. They ordered beer and whatever was cooking. Ten minutes later, as the food arrived, Julia, Tam, and Chen walked by the window and a few minutes later they had pulled up chairs and crowded around the small table. Julia displayed her new hat, leather, with a wide brim. She and Tam also had bought new boots.

Two tables away, four men were deep in conversation. One patron, a man of apparent late twenties with a long black beard--braided and hanging to his belly--eyed the others. "I told you and I'll tell you again. The right words leave me when trying to describe it. I felt like an insect looking at a giant oak from the ground. What wonders would an insect assume about a tree that might take it fifty lifetimes to explore?"

"All I asked was your impression, friend," an older man across from him said.

Caleb and the others stopped their discussion of traveling attire and listened in.

Julia leaned in close to Captain Newton. "Sound familiar?"

"Yes, it does," the captain said, glancing aside to the four men.

Julia said, "That man with the long black beard arrived here in Havana about a week ago. He visited the great city and is on his way back to Brazil."

"How do you know?" Caleb asked, turning his chair a little so he could covertly watch the men.

"The whole town is talking about it, apparently. The shop owner where I bought my boots told me this morning."

Tam said loudly. "And you have to go, too. The messenger said so."

Caleb cringed. "Easy, Tam. Not so loud."

Julia pulled Tam closer and whispered to him, "I don't think we're supposed to tell the whole world, Tam."

A woman at the table next to them turned to them. "Are you the man that was called? Did you just come in with Captain Newt?" she trailed off when she saw Caleb's face. "I apologize for intruding, friend." Abashed, she turned back to her food.

Caleb took a deep breath and turned in his chair. "That's okay, ma'am. No harm done. I'm Caleb Carson. Yes, I was called. No big deal. We're on our way to find out what it's all about." He shook her hand.

"I see," she murmured.

"I fail to see how it could be a small thing," the man with the black beard said, standing and stepping over to their table. A few seconds later all eyes in the room were on Caleb's table.

Caleb raised both hands. Chuckling uncomfortably, he said, "We're still trying to figure it out."

Black Beard pulled up a chair and sat close. "Greeting, Captain Newton and madam."

Julia nodded to him, as did the captain.

"I hope I'm not intruding, but I heard about you this morning. You are also the man who ran to mountains, Si, I mean, yes?"

Caleb's brow rose. "How did you know that?"

Black Beard paused. "I have forgotten my manners. Please, may I begin again? My name is Juan San Marco De Guez. I heard of you this morning and I also saw you running this morning. Actually, you ran right past me while I had morning coffee with my friends. We thought you were on a great journey with your backpack."

"How did you know I went to the mountains?"

Marco sighed dramatically. "I have been blessed with knowing things others don't notice."

Julia asked Juan San Marco, "I heard you are returning from the great city?"

"Yes, madam."

"How long were you there, if I may ask?"

He put his hands together as if in prayer and breathed deep. "No problem. I always say a prayer when asked about my journey. I was there eighty-three years."

"And you can't describe it?" Julia asked.

"Oh, I can describe it. I cannot describe it *well*."

Captain Newton remarked, " I docked at the Western Gate, the one that opens into the Mediterranean Lake just northeast of Bengasi. I didn't go in. Didn't want to leave my boat. I saw the Wall and the Western Gate. I also saw the light streaming through the clouds from the sky."

Juan San Marco nodded vigorously, his long black beard wavering in his lap. "Yes, the light from the tower. It covers the whole city and is too bright to those not prepared."

"Tell me about the tower," Caleb said.

"The tower, my friend, is the center of it all. All power, all purpose, all wisdom comes from the tower. I didn't believe, at first, what the citizens said about the tower—until I approached it." He laughed quietly for a moment. "I thought I was a spiritual man. I was a priest in my former life, you know. I had many grand delusions about what spiritual means. I thought I was good. I thought I was better than most, even. In my arrogance I had made an oath to not cut my beard," he lifted the black hair and let it fall back to his lap, "till I was able to stand inside that place. I sat at the entrance to the tower and cried for three days because I couldn't enter. The doors were open, and I was free to walk right in, but my conscience spoke to me more strongly the closer I got to the tower. I was three easy steps from the threshold…"

"And?" Julia asked.

"You see, only those who see themselves as Jesus sees them can enter. I simply wasn't ready to enter in. I couldn't say to myself, yet, that I still fell short of his goodness. Do you understand?"

They sat quietly and listened.

"I longed to enter the tower, to experience the wonders of his presence up close, but my feet said, 'not yet.'"

"After that, I met many citizens who lived near the tower and studied at the university there. Many of them had entered into the lower parts of the tower.

"Do you understand what the tower is now? God, Himself, is at the top of the tower. We can climb the tower—there are many grand staircases, they say, and many places to stop and be refreshed. Angels minister to mendicants as they travel upward. We can climb upward any time we want, but we must overcome ourselves first. The holy prophets of old and the twelve are up there."

Caleb listened quietly. "Bloody he..." He shut his lips tightly, shaking his head. He thought, I'm supposed to go in there? There's no way I'll get within a hundred miles of the place.

Juan San Marco said to Caleb, "A messenger came to your village and called you by name. What else can you do, but go?"

"Go the other direction," Caleb said.

The former priest said, "Some have, but eventually they all feel His absence. He made us for a purpose. Finding our purpose is how we find peace."

"What about the rest of the city? I take it you traveled?" One of the listeners in the crowd asked.

"Yes. It was my fourth year in the Great City that I approached the tower. While I was there, Jesus heard my prayer and knew my grief there. He gave me a gift--to understand certain things more clearly. It has helped me greatly.

"I traveled almost eighty years from one wall of the city to the next. It was wonderful. You must understand the holy city is more like a country. Some day it will be filled with the resurrected from wall to wall, but it is not finished, yet. We are to finish building and furnishing it. It is one of our ways of growing.

"Many there had climbed partway up the tower. They all had such wonderful experiences. I eventually realized I needed to come home for a while."

The room went silent. Many of the other patrons understood Marco's grief while at the tower and his decision to come home. Home is where great decisions need to be made and, sometimes, great discoveries. The waiter silently moved among the patrons, topping drinks and gathering plates.

"What now, Juan San Marco?" Captain Newton asked.

He breathed deep. "Ah. Now I return home to my sanctuary in the hills, a familiar place, the place where I lived my great lie. Now my eyes are more open, if not my heart. It will take time to mend the heartache of understanding the extent of my imperfection. I have many friends there at the monastery. I'm not sure how, but I believe I can feel them even from here."

"Then you must be on your journey?" Julia said.

"Yes. And with that, I'll bid you all…" He faced Caleb. "Go. I believe you are a man who embraces challenge. Remember what you learned from your short journey to the mountains nearby. When God calls you, He will give you the way to overcome all obstacles."

The men stood and Caleb put out a hand. Juan ignored the hand and wrapped his arms around Caleb and hugged him hard. "God will be with you and my prayers, my brother. Look me up after you have reached the top," he whispered. He let him go and stepped back, then with a quick bow to the others turned and left the cafe, long black beard waving in the air.

The next morning, they were all aboard and on their way down the river as the sun rose over the trees. The captain announced they would see little sign of civilization for the next three weeks as they were going out into open wilderness. The river would take them east past where the Caribbean used to be dotted with islands. Now the islands were merely mountains in a wilderness of jungle, savannah of high grass, and many lakes. The *Mercy* chugged along on idle using only enough engine power to steer in the slowly flowing current.

Caleb, Jake, Julia, Chen, and Tam were sitting on the upper deck. Someone had pulled out a deck of cards and Jake was teaching the others the rules of the game.

"Okay, my mates, you just need to remember the rules and you're good."

"I don't remember this game, and I'm from nearly the same time as you," Julia said, holding the cards up and trying to hide them from prying eyes.

"Probably because you're from the south of England and I'm from the Scottish Highlands," Jake said, "though I did spend a lot of time in London."

"What is this a picture of?" Tam held a card up to Jake.

"That's a beaver," Jake said. "They have flat tails and make dams in rivers."

"What's a dam?" Tam asked.

"I'll explain later," Caleb said. "Am I supposed to discard two cards now?"

Jake nodded. "Yep. Those are the rules. I know because I made them up myself."

"These cards are strange, too," Julia said. "Did you make them, too?"

"Had them made by a professional. The only pack like them on this whole world. Guaranteed unique."

"I believe you." Chen studied his cards and put two down. Then put another down.

"Are you supposed to do that?" Julia asked.

Chen shrugged. "I think so. This game is similar to one I've seen."

"Good move, Chen," Jake said. "You're obviously a master card player. Just don't make me look bad. I'm trying to impress you guys with my inventive mind."

Captain Newton was in the steering cabin above them as usual. He sounded a quick puff on the boat's air horn.

Caleb pulled his cards close to his chest and looked up at him through the open front window. The captain pointed forward and shouted down at them. "Around this bend, coming up about now."

Caleb looked out ahead over the water. A few seconds later wooded riverbank gave way to open swampy grassland. Caleb stood, then Tam.

"I'll be..." Caleb struggled for a word, "something."

"What are they?" Tam asked.

Jake pretended to yawn. "Oh, they're just extinct brontosauruses enjoying a day in the swamp. No big deal. Let's play cards."

Julia put her cards down, as did the others except Jake, then with a pretended frown he put his down too.

They approached slowly, the boat angling closer, the captain wary of shallow water.

The giant animals' long necks arched up seventy feet into the air from fat walrus-like bodies on tree trunk legs. There were eight of them. The largest turned his head toward them and bellowed a low warble.

"I don't think he likes us," Tam said.

"He's letting us know he sees us, is all," Jake assured him.

"They're a lot bigger than I thought," Caleb said. "I used to have a cellphone. I would love to get a picture of them."

"If anyone wants to see them all he has to do is come here and look," Chen said.

Caleb pursed his lips. "That seems to be a very oriental way of looking at it."

They stood by the rail and watched the previously extinct animals as the boat slowly coasted by until they were out of sight around a bend.

CHAPTER SIX

A few days later, Captain Newton called for a break in their travels. They slowed at the entrance to a tributary flowing from the east. They had angled north a few weeks ago and the landscape had changed gradually. Caleb noticed the riverbanks were getting higher and the jungle was beginning to give way to deciduous, broadleaf trees and less vines. Captain Newton turned the boat into the narrow tributary. The boat's motor rose in pitch as they moved a quarter mile upstream till a wooden dock hove into view.

The captain cut the engines and called down. "Let's tie-up and meet at the plank."

Caleb and the others met the captain at the rail. "What place is this?" Caleb asked.

"We need to stock up on potable water and this place has the freshest water I know of," Captain Newton said.

He pointed upriver and due east. "It doesn't seem like it, but we're about two hundred miles from the African continent. We'll travel north for two more weeks, then turn east into the Strait of Gibraltar and head into the Mediterranean lakes."

"Is the Med dried up like the Atlantic?" Julia asked.

"Pretty much. The Balearic, Tyrhenian, and Ionian seas are big lakes now joined by various tributaries. The Mediterranean Sea starts past Malta and is the largest body of water I know of, but it's not really a sea anymore. The western gate opens right into the Med' a few miles north of what used to be called Cyrene, but now is a major town, what with being so close to the gate."

"Is that the gate we will enter through?" Tam asked.

Captain Newton shrugged. "It's the only one with a dock right on the water. So, I suppose so."

After the crewmen tied up, a wide giant of a man ambled down the dock, waving. "Ho, brother. It's been a while." The dock vibrated with each step he took.

Caleb watched, fascinated that the dock didn't just cave in. The man must have been seven feet tall and shaped much like a whiskey barrel.

Captain Newton waved back. "Gelder, we're on our way to the great city. Thought we'd refresh ourselves, restock and try your food while we're here."

The big man stopped at the side of the ship. The dock stopped quivering.

"So, has the whole world heard of my cooking yet? It is inevitable, you know."

"You seem to enjoy it enough for three men," the captain said.

"Ah, yes you noticed," he laughed.

"Let's go to sturdy ground and we can discuss my needs and you can show my friends your home." The captain waved toward the very large house and manicured, yard up a low hill fifty yards away.

The home seemed to be taken from the pages of a great picture book of legends, part Viking longhouse, and part Hobbit earth dwelling, with another part Chinese traditional wavy hip roof.

Long square beams extended out from the eves and plastered exterior walls displayed paintings of landscapes from around the world.

As they drew closer, Captain Newton remarked, "I see you've added another scene."

"Yes, I was inspired by the Greeks and Romans. Just a subtle touch, though. Do you see right here?" Gelder extended a sausage finger toward the wall.

Julia stepped closer. "Yes, the arch, right?"

"Good, I was concerned. I started over many times."

They entered the home. It was cool and spartan. The open-beamed roof allowed light to filter down. The glassed-in windows were open allowing a breeze to blow across the room. Medieval arched beams supported the entrance, rough in texture, but soft to the touch.

As they entered the living room Caleb noticed one wall was covered with a canvas sheet hung on pegs. He pointed to the wall. "Is that one of your paintings in progress?"

"Ah, yes. I've been working on it for years, but it is a continuing project. I can't seem to capture the feeling I'm looking for."

They walked through the home down a wide hallway leading to a veranda in the back extending out to a long, wide, tree covered glade.

"What do you think?" Gelder said.

"Beautiful," they chorused.

Chen asked, "How do you keep it so tidy?"

"I don't actually do much of the upkeep around here. That's the work of the forest people."

Jake asked, "Forest people?"

"Oh, yes. They live all around in the forest. Evidently, they enjoy coming by and fixing up the place. Have been for about two hundred years or so. Many of these trees here, they planted. The whole design is theirs. They have other places in the forest like this. In exchange, I cook a feast for them on special occasions."

"Nice arrangement," Jake said.

Gelder waved at chairs and cushions." Make yourselves comfortable. I was about to start work in the kitchen when I heard that unmistakable sound of the captain's riverboat. I'll cook for us."

An hour later they all filed into a massive dining room. Murals covered the walls. Some were of the forest people, short, staid, and poised, dressed in colorful rough fabric.

The food was wonderful, as they expected and the conversation colorful and wide ranging. It seemed Gelder, also, had spent many years traveling after his rebirth.

"Does every wall in your home have a painting on it?" Tam asked.

"Yes, I've enjoyed surrounding myself with a rendering of places I've traveled," Gelder said.

"What about the mystery painting behind the canvas?" Caleb asked.

Captain Newton raised a hand. "Let's not pressure our host. Perhaps it's more of a personal nature."

Gelder chewed the last bite and put down his fork. "Not at all. It's that I only display what I've finished. Come, I'll show it to you. You aren't the first to ask." They rose and walked into the living room.

Gelder approached the canvas and grabbed a corner. "Ready?"

They all stood in front of the canvas. Gelder whipped the canvas off with a "Ta'da."

Caleb instantly knew what he saw. Although he'd never been there, he knew it must be a view of New Jerusalem from high altitude--perhaps a mountain or a plane at five thousand feet.

"Wow," Julia breathed.

"This is amazing."

Caleb stared but couldn't identify much of the detail. He saw a white band below, straight as an arrow, extending away into a thin line along the contours of the land. In the distance, giant patches of white and gray blocks grew tall intricate patterns interspersed with green. Further away the land seemed to rise, then he realized the size of the structures became wider and rose higher the closer they were to the tower.

The tower rose like a giant metal candle, tapering gradually to disappear out of sight into space, through all layers of the atmosphere, past the radiation belt and the thermosphere. Three different layers of clouds floated in static display in mid-swirl as if rotating around its four faces. There were openings in the sides of the tower at various altitudes up and down the face like dark dots of pepper. White dots flew away and swirled around the edifice. They could be flies buzzing around a candle in any other context.

"Where did you take this?" Caleb said, then realized his mistake. This painting appeared to be a photo it was so detailed. "I mean, where were you when you saw this?"

"I was halfway up Mount Olympus. But there is something you must understand. The city does not look like this, now. While up on the mountain Our Lord gave me a vision of what it will look like when finished. This was my vision. The great city's wall was only forty miles from me, and I saw much open space with scattered towns within the confines of the great walls. I stayed up there three weeks and thought on my vision and questioned whether I was worthy to paint it."

"Do you know what those white specks high up the tower will be?" Jake asked.

"I have been told they would be flying craft, like a dirigible," Gelder said.

"Did you enter the city?" Julia asked.

"No."

Those colorful blocks and those green places, what are they?" Julia asked.

"Great buildings where the citizens live, and the green patches are parks and gardens. The sparkles are from the many rooftops. You can see more detail in the villages and towns that are closer."

A few minutes later, Gelder asked, "So, what do you think? Some say this painting is finished. I'm not so sure. I feel I've missed something important."

Chen remarked. "I agree. I see the structure and function. I feel the distance and magnitude of effort to create this city. Pardon, but I don't feel its purpose."

Gelder stared at Chen a moment, then let the canvas drop to cover the painting. "You're right, of course. The great city is nothing if not purpose. I'm at wit's end on how to give it that."

"You must visit the city," Captain Newton said. "I think that will be the only way to find out how. You must experience that purpose yourself."

Deflated, Gelder said, "Let's retire to the veranda." On the way down the hallway, Chen asked, "Friend Gelder, this painting here," he waved at the wall they passed. "Did you go there?"

"Yes."

"And the other paintings, did you go there, too? Did you walk the land and know the people?"

"I see where you wish my thoughts to go. Yes, I did experience those places."

"That is why they touch my soul, "Chen said.

Gelder stopped. "Look at me. Do I look like a man who can travel? It would disrupt my life too much. Where would I cook? What about my forest friends?"

The captain quickly interjected, "We understand completely. No need to explain."

When they reached the veranda Gelder sat down among cushions and stared out at the forest.

Captain Newton said, "Thank you for your hospitality, Gelder. We should see about supplying the boat."

With a quick thanks from all, they left Gelder to his thoughts.

The next morning, they had almost finished loading the boat by the time the sun was above the tree line. The water canisters had been brought ashore and filled. Crates of food had been loaded aboard and the last of the crew and passengers stood about on the lower deck waiting for the captain to return from saying his farewells.

Caleb was in conversation with the ship's cook and other crew when one of the crewmen pointed up the hill toward the house. A small crowd of forest folk was walking down the hill carrying boxes, the captain and Gelder with them. As they approached, the captain yelled, "Make way for cargo."

The crewmen scrambled out onto the deck and helped the forest folk load the boxes. On the solid ground, the captain and Gelder had a short conversation and the captain patted Gelder on the arm and turned toward the boat, then Gelder followed.

As the captain stepped aboard, he said, "We have a new passenger. Everyone welcome Gelder aboard."

Caleb smiled as the crew and some of the passengers let out a cheer. The large man stepped aboard with the help of the crew. Caleb was a little surprised the boat didn't dip at least a little from his weight. The captain climbed up to the upper deck. The whistle sounded, the steam engine puffed, and the wheels began a slow churn as the boat backed away from the dock and began a slow turn to follow the tributary back to the main river.

Three weeks later, the travelers had reached sight of the African coastline of Morocco. As usual, the original coastline was a line of hills and cliffs in the distance. The land the rest of the way down to the Med' River was covered in dryland scrub increasingly denser the closer to the river. At the riverbank, palm trees lined the water's edge.

"This looks a lot like the way I remember the Nile," Caleb said.

"So true." Jake and Caleb stood at the rail and tossed peanut shells into the water and watched fish rise up to nibble.

Lowering his voice, Jake said, "No aspersion on the boat's cook, but I think the food has dramatically improved the last three weeks."

"Maybe when we get to more open water, we'll get a catch of tuna or swordfish if they're still around. The captain said the Balearic Islands are on the other side of the Strait of Gibraltar. A large lake is there."

"I've had swordfish. It's good."

Caleb pondered aloud. "So, we travel east to the Balearic, cross it, continue past Sicily to the Ionian Lake Basin into the largest lake at the southern tip of Greece, and then we'll be a couple of days from the wall."

"About a week and a half according to my reckoning," Jake said as he dumped the remainder of his peanut shells into the water.

"We'll see Gibraltar soon," Julia approached them.

"So, it seems. I've not seen it before." Jake said.

Julia leaned on the rail. "Gibralter has a local ruler. He's talking about building a bridge across from Europe to Africa. It's only a river running through here now, only about four hundred yards wide."

"Then we'll not get close to the big rock I remember seeing pictures of. I'm not disappointed," Caleb said.

"Still worried about the city?" she asked.

"Oh yeah. Never off my mind."

She put a hand on his arm. "You'll get answers soon. It won't be long."

Jake announced. "I'm going to visit the cook. See you about."

Waving Jake off, Caleb turned toward the rail, leaned on it, and watched the palm trees pass. Julia did the same.

After a moment of silence, Caleb said, "I had a dream last night. Or maybe it was a memory. I'm not sure."

"Oh?"

"It was about my outfit, the men I lead."

"Was it awful?"

"No, not really. It was about one of my last conflicts. A skirmish, really. Nothing big. But I did lose a couple of men to snipers before we took them out."

"Sounds very dangerous."

"Yeah, I suppose so, but that was our business, fighting for other people."

"You mean you were a mercenary?" she asked.

Caleb cringed inside a little. "I'm afraid so. I'm not proud of it."

"Caleb, this is heaven. We learn not to judge. I've received my memories and I know I have no ground on which to judge."

"By 'memory', you mean memory of the judgment?"

She nodded.

"It must have been intense."

She frowned, then smiled and frowned again, a little flustered. "I've thought much on those days—my days standing before the Lord in judgement. I have so many mixed emotions. It was exhilarating and scary, tearful, and remorseful, many things, then, at the end--peaceful. After that I waited to find what my rewards would be, that is, what station I would occupy in this new society. I am very satisfied I was judged--perfectly."

The day passed quietly as Caleb enjoyed the scenery. When the sun set, he found his bunk and fell asleep instantly, as usual. Ten minutes into sleep the dreams started.

He remembered.

It was early morning. The sun was barely shining through dense upper branches of distant trees. His convoy struggled up a rocky dirt road.

They'd passed the border not more than a mile back and so far, the enemy hadn't presented themselves. Captain Caleb Carson, Lt. Mosely, and Sergeant Ramon sat in the cab of the fourth truck.

Sgt. Ramon swayed with the roll of the truck as it hit a dip in the road. "I'm surprised they let us get this far without showing themselves."

"It's a trap for sure." Lt. Mosely hawked up a bit of blood from an earlier skirmish where he got hit in the face by a truck door and spit out the window.

"Yeah, well, it's only a trap if you don't know it's there. An ambush is different. That, you don't see coming."

As the words left his mouth, Caleb heard the whump of distant mortars. "Call ahead, full speed. We got to get over this hill." He glanced to his men. "Now, this is an ambush."

The convoy struggled up the hill and crested it as the first mortar found its range. The second truck rocked on its suspension as another mortar landed ten feet from its back tire.

"Call the general. Tell him we've made contact." Caleb leaned out the passenger side window and scanned the rocks and sparse growth. He saw no enemy out to a thousand yards.

"Over this hill should be flat land. We need to pick up speed or we're screwed. Call in an airstrike. Tell them you'll have coordinates in one minute."

Caleb put the binoculars down. As they crested the hill, they were presented with rocky open savanna and a straight road. A hundred yards away, the enemy had laid large rocks across the road, behind which machine gun fire began in earnest.

"Take out those machine guns and go around those rocks. We can't stop now." Caleb heard the rasp of a SAW, his company's biggest machine gun, as the forward truck let loose with a stream of lead. The rocks ahead powdered as chips flew. The enemy hunkered down. As Caleb's truck passed the rocks and deadly enemy, he heard the truck in the rear explode. He glanced in his rearview mirror and saw a fireball and truck parts fly.

"Damn it. Tell everyone to conserve ammo. We just lost a quarter of ours. Call in a strike, best estimate."

They made it another quarter mile and the lead truck exploded and flipped over landing on the side of the road.

Lt. Mosely held a radio to his head. "Captain, Wilson says there's a tank out there somewhere."

Caleb's heart lurched. He then knew this entire company, including the general, had been screwed by someone high up the political ladder. "Abort the mission, orderly retreat. Stop this truck and bring up our last two SAWs."

Caleb pulled out his map and traced the riverbed angling west from their position. It was a good thing he'd studied this territory thoroughly. "Tell Wilson…" Caleb took the radio. "Wilson, take the lead, follow the riverbed a mile and quarter, and cut south. You'll be a half-mile from the border. No. Just do it. That's an order."

Lt. Mosely and Sgt. Ramon finished setting up one of the SAW machine guns. In case the enemy decided to attack with infantry they set about laying down suppressor fire in a wide arc. Wilson drove past them as fast as he reasonably could in the direction they came from. Once past, he drove off the road into the savanna, headed for the riverbed.

Caleb counted seven vehicles rushing past, then tapped the Sargent on the shoulder. "Okay, let's get out of here." As he turned to speak to the lieutenant, he heard the whistle of an incoming mortar, he felt tremendous pressure, the air turned red--then blackness.

For a few seconds, all Caleb remembered was the flash. Then the memories came back in a rush. He was laying on the ground, the truck that he, Lieutenant Mosely, and Master Sergeant Ramon had been riding in, lay on its side ripped almost in two. Caleb held up his hands and looked down at his feet. All his body parts were present. He heard a sound and twisted around to see Ramon approaching.

"What the hell happened, Captain?"

"We were hit by a mortar and our truck blew up, I think."

"Then why aren't we dead?" Ramon looked around. In every direction was a smoky haze. The uphill desert road they'd been traveling was pocked by craters and the immediate environment was still, the air wavering under a hot sun.

Ramon helped Caleb to his feet, and they walked around the truck and found the lieutenant on his knees reaching for a rifle.

"Mosely," Caleb said as they stepped over to the lieutenant.

"The truck is busted but good," Mosely said.

"Yeah, it's time to walk, then. Let's find weapons and look for survivors."

They all heard the scrape of a shoe sole on gravel. "You won't need to do that."

They turned quickly to see a tall man in desert camouflage standing ten feet away. His hair was short, black, and curly. His eyes shone bright and green. He said, "Your battle is over. It's time to leave the battlefield."

Caleb took one step forward. "I don't recognize your uniform. Who would you be and why do we need to leave?"

"I'm your guardian and you three are dead."

In a flash, Caleb, Mosely, and Ramon stood at the crest of a hill before the gatehouse of a great fortress. It was of white stone, gleaming under a clear blue sky. A breeze blew cool around them. Caleb looked around in all directions. Behind them the road they stood in the middle of ended a hundred yards back and continued as untouched grassy hills. Before them lay the fortress and beyond its walls a green valley and many structures as far as the eye could see. The doors of the fortress began opening with a rumble and a guard with a long spear and full medieval battle dress stepped out and beckoned. As the doors swung wide, other guards stepped out and lined the entrance. Then the guard captain removed his helmet. With a smile, he said, "Welcome to Paradise."

"What is this place?" Caleb asked.

He got no answer, except the shrill whistle of a boat's horn. Caleb opened his eyes, blinking, rolled out of his bunk, and sat in a daze pondering what he'd just experienced. He heard the muffled whistle of an answer from a distant passing ship across the water.

"It seemed so darn real," he said aloud, to the wall inches from his face. Then standing, he stretched his shoulders as he made his way outside to see the sun rising over arid land.

"Here's sleeping beauty." Jake approached with a mug of hot coffee. "More where I got this." He raised the mug a few inches.

Caleb stared at him.

"Hey, you awake, yet?"

"Yeah, just getting my bearings. I had a whopper of a dream," Caleb said.

"Oh yeah? You can tell all of us at breakfast, which is ready now. I was coming to toss you out of bed to join the living, but I see you're almost awake. let's go fill up for the coming day."

The others were already there when Jake and Caleb walked in. They served themselves from the small bar and sat on benches bolted to the deck.

Julia, Chen, Gelder, Tam, and Captain Newton were already tucking in.

"You slept a long time," Julia said.

"Yeah, I had a good rest, considering I got blown up."

"What do you mean?" Chen asked.

"I dreamed I was with my men. My convoy was traveling across the desert and my truck got hit by a mortar. Me and my two buddies died. Finally came to a big valley filled with a big bustling city," Caleb said, while forking breakfast into his mouth.

"Was there a fortress?" Captain Newton asked.

"Yeah, how...?

Captain Newton said, while chewing, "It was a memory, not a dream--maybe both. We've all been there. You'll remember it all eventually, but I'm surprised you remember any of it. It was a lot of years before I remembered any of it."

"That place was real?" Caleb asked, putting down his fork.

"I remember a lot of my time there," Chen said.

"Where is there?"

Gelder leaned back in his chair, laced his fingers together, and propped them on his ample belly. "My friend, before you woke up here you lived in a place called Paradise. We all did. I remember much of it. I lived there about three-hundred years, and I have many fond memories of my time there. It's where I learned to cook; you can learn a lot about cooking in three hundred years."

Caleb looked around at his friends. "You all were there?"

"It was a temporary place to live while the Lord cleansed the earth and refurbished it," Captain Newton said.

"Well? Where was it?"

Jake pointed a finger down toward the deck. "Somewhere inside the world were four chambers for those who die. One for the righteous and three for the unrighteous. But after the Lord rose from the dead, he brought all the righteous out and moved paradise up there somewhere. You were covered by Our Lord's blood, so you went to the good place up there and now you're here."

"Wow." Caleb raked both hands through his hair. "This is my first memory, then. How long was I there?"

"I can tell you, but it is usually better to wait for the Lord to send you the memories," Jake said.

"It sure would be nice to know."

"Okay," Jake said. "What was the year you were born?"

"Nineteen seventy-five."

"Ah, I need more information. Who was king at the time?" Jake asked.

"King?"

"Yeah, king of America."

"There wasn't any king. We had a president," Caleb said, chuckling.

"Oh, I see you lived pre-millennial. For some reason, I thought you lived after that. That means you were in paradise about four-teen-hundred years. Something like that."

Caleb laughed. They all watched him till he stopped laughing. "You're serious?" he asked.

"Yeah, you'll remember most of it eventually. You'll have lots of good memories," Jake promised.

Julia put her spoon down. "Caleb, it seems things--spiritual things--are happening to you faster than normal. I don't know what it means, but maybe it has to do with your calling."

"Like the life you had in paradise..." Chen began to say.

"...Or your memories of something that happened then, is needed now," Julia finished.

CHAPTER SEVEN

Two days later they rounded the southern end of Sicily. From there to the east lay the largest lake in the middle east. It was deep water all the way to the western gate which was situated south of Greece a few miles off the coast of North Africa. Captain Newton wanted to resupply, so they sailed north for a few hours and stopped at Syracuse which was still located close to the water, but hundreds of feet high up a cliff.

They stopped and explored for a day. It was there Julia first heard word of her mother.

That night, Caleb had another dream. It was a continuation of the first one and he remembered entering the city of Paradise with his men where the righteous waited for judgement day.

The next morning, he told the others of it, and they all reminisced long about their own time there. The first dream seemed to set a pattern for the next two weeks as they traveled east toward New Jerusalem.

It was afternoon and as they were all getting back aboard, Julia announced to the group she heard that her mother was somewhere in the holy city. Later, standing by the rail, she, Caleb, and Jake discussed their foray onto the island.

Julia said, "The cobbler told me he was from the same neighborhood as we were in the first life. He went back to London to live for a while and met Mother there. He said she appears as young as a fresh flower. I think he may have had a thing for her."

"Going to look for her?" Jake asked.

"I don't know where to start."

The captain ambled by and stopped. "You can ask for help."

Julia turned to him. "Does the city have a program for finding people?"

"Not that I know of," the captain said. "I mean you can pray. Maybe the Lord will give you a few clues on where to start. I've heard from others it seems to work that way."

The captain turned to Caleb, "Any new thoughts about your expanding memories?"

"Yeah, I'm starting to remember people and places."

"Good. I'm very curious as to why your memories are coming much faster than most. But I guess we'll know in good time." He nodded and walked away.

The day wore on. Rain threatened from the eastern sky, even though, through the clouds, thin streamers of light still cast warm sparkles on the open water.

Jake pointed at the light spots on the water. "That's from the tower and we're still about, oh, fifteen hundred miles from it. I can't picture anything that big, except maybe Mount Everest."

"Mount Everest would be small in comparison," Julia said.

"So true," Jake said, then frowned at a memory. "I met a guy once who walked all the way around the tower's base. He said it took him six weeks. Of course, the northern face of the base is heavily populated being close to the entrance. Lots of high buildings and other structures and such, some even built right against the tower. He said it's something like fifty miles by fifty miles. He was a very chatty fellow. Probably spent most of his time talking instead of walking."

"Still a really big place," Julia said.

"Then you go inside. The first floor is huge. The whole thing is one big park. The holy trees are there and they say you will hardly believe how good the water is--invigorating. The ceiling is half mile high, and it rains inside sometimes."

"A park forty miles by forty miles. Sounds like the garden of Eden," Caleb said.

"Got it in on the first guess, "Jake said, "You've read the bible, right?"

"Yeah, a long time ago."

"Take my word for it. It's big and it's the Garden of Eden or I'm not the Jake you all admire."

Julia put her arm around Jake's shoulder. "Well, it must be, because we admire you so much."

They all chuckled.

Tam and Chen approached. Tam said, "Captain Newton said we're two days from the western gate."

"Oh?"

"Yeah, we're going to dock there for a day. A town is there."

"Where's Gelder? What's he planning for lunch?"

"I don't know, but he says he plans on staying on the *Mercy* and getting off at the next gate, the one in Greece. He offered to make a special dinner for us before we leave."

"I'm going to miss his cooking,"Chen said with a sigh,"He does good oriental."

"And American."

"And English," Julia said.

That night the sky cleared for a spell and the stars shined bright. Caleb, Julia, Jake, Tam, and Gelder all sat up on the top deck on lounge chairs the captain had procured at their last stop. Chen leaned against the rail and stared out at the open water. "You all know I'm from the Orient because of my straight eyes and my accent. What you don't know is my life up to the very end was ruled by the bushido. I was samurai as was my father and my grandfather. It was my air and my water.

"When I was young, perhaps seven years, a missionary from Europe came to my village. I remember him as very tall and broad shouldered. He had golden hair down to his shoulders. To us he seemed a barbarian, unkempt and dirty, having walked from the coast to our mountain pass. His demeanor put off the adults. He never seemed to bow properly, and he talked incessantly. His accent was strange as were his words. He talked of peace the way we did of war. He talked of war the way we did of peace. In the end, our liege ordered him killed. His words aroused anger for most, but for some of us, his words were a door to another way of thinking. They sank deep within me, and I accepted them, though I didn't know it then.

"On the day of my death the weather was cool and humid. Gray fog surrounded the mountains. We were attacked as the sun rose. They came at us with the sun at their backs which, as you know, gave them the initial advantage. We couldn't determine their numbers quickly enough. I fought two before me and in the first few seconds of the fight a third Samurai from our neighboring valley thrust me through. He moved on and for ten minutes I lay in the damp grass and shuddered from the pain. I had many thoughts of my family and I worried for them."

Chen paused for a moment and looked out at the passing water. "I learned a lesson from my death; our deepest desires come to the surface in moments when we know our time is at an end. The missionary's words came back to me clearly, then. I embraced them and died."

They were silent for a while. The engines thumped and chugged as the paddles washed the air, leaving churning foam in the *Mercy's* wake.

Chen said. "I had a very dramatic death. A good one, I think. Those ten minutes of pain were worth it."

He continued, "It seems our Lord brings us here to a place far from our original homes. I was raised in Japan, but reborn in Wichita, Kansas. It was very different, indeed. Perhaps the reason is we need to take a physical journey as well as a spiritual one. I eventually made my way to Japan, but as a very different person. At my rebirth, I still considered myself samurai. It was all I knew. I was reborn in a small wooden church outside a village of three hundred. They were as we are now. We are at home in our cleansed world, but we are still sojourners. We still must learn and grow; that will never stop and that is my greatest joy. I have been here one hundred twenty-seven years and have not been bored for a minute."

"Amen to that."

"Amen."

Chen pointed to the eastern sky and the golden glow above the clouds. "I came from the 'land of the rising sun,' but that is the land of never-ending light."

"Well told, brother Chen," Gelder said. "Now, it's my turn." Gelder pushed himself from his chair and strode about the deck for a moment, collecting his thoughts.

He said, "I was a professional wrestler. I traveled about Europe giving a try to anyone who took my challenge. I never once tried to cook as much as an egg. I was a pretty good wrestler. 'Gelder the Grave' was my stage name. Yes, I know it sounds ridiculous.

"Anyway, my life was undramatic till my last bout. I was in Paris and facing a young, homegrown Parisian guy about my size. Who would have guessed they made Frenchmen that big? So, we start wrestling, but then the guy starts throwing punches. He hit like a hammer. Well, I could do that, too. I wasn't a one trick act. So, I hit him back and down he goes. He gets up grinning. Evidently, I was the first to knock him on his butt. So, we go at it for a good ten minutes. The youth gets up three times. Then he gets a good one on me and I drop. At the time my youth was a distant memory. I really felt that one. I got up and declared him the winner. I didn't want to be hit like that again. That's why I wrestled.

"After the bout, we hugged each other, winner, and loser, and had drinks at a local bar. Later I had a heart attack outside on the cobblestone street. I lay on my back surrounded by people.

"Someone put a hand on my shoulder, and I looked up to see a tall man smiling at me. He glowed like he was opaque. He said, 'Come home.'"

"So, here I am. I don't know why or how I made it here. Somehow in the broken life I led, I found Jesus. I still don't know, but I'm glad I'm here and I praise our merciful Lord. Then I spent three-hundred years in paradise learning how to cook and learning I could paint."

"Amen to you, too," Caleb said.

"I would never have guessed," Julia said.

We all have stories," Jake said.

"Yes, we do," Caleb said. "And I really appreciate hearing yours, but I'm beat. I'm calling it a day. See you all in the morning" He waved as he headed to the ladder that took him down to his bunk.

That night Caleb dreamed, as usual. But this time it was more vivid and emotionally charged; he remembered Anna Hudson. And, for him, heaven changed.

Caleb woke with a start, jumped from his bunk, and paced the small cabin for a moment, then throwing on his clothes, he stepped out onto the deck and stood by the rail, gripping it tightly and staring into the night sky and the dim golden haze to the east.

Anna, she must be here, he thought. No one was up yet, and he didn't feel like being alone, so he climbed up the ladder to the pilot's station to find Captain Newton lounging at the wheel and watching the approaching sunrise.

"Captain." Caleb stood at the doorway.

Captain Newton turned his head and nodded. "Couldn't sleep?"

"Yeah."

"Come in."

Caleb sat on a stool bolted to the floor and joined him looking out at the dark water.

"Another dream?"

"Yeah."

"It must have been a good one because you seem to be ready to get off and walk the rest of the way."

"I remembered someone very special to me."

"I know. Anna Hudson."

Caleb gripped the chair. "I should be used to this by now."

"The Lord told me last night. I had a vision about her... and you." The captain stayed relaxed at the wheel. "She's in the City. She's been called, too, but you're supposed to relax and trust that everything is in hand. That's what I was told."

Caleb said, "It all came together. I remember almost everything. Not my death, but my time in paradise."

"My, that's a lot of remembering. Best to take it easy and let it all settle in. You feel like a different person, right?"

Caleb nodded. "Yes, all those memories. All the things I learned for all those years. They seemed to pass so swiftly. Seemed like a short time."

"That's what I experienced, too."

"How long before we get to the western gate?"

"Still another two days. This old paddlewheel wasn't designed for speed."

The captain took his mind off Anna as best he could for the next few hours by reminiscing on his own life. As the sun came up, they heard the cook banging pots and pans.

"You might as well get some breakfast. They'll all be up shortly," the captain said. "You can miss the rush. While you're at it, ask Sam to fix me the usual, would you?"

Caleb was back fifteen minutes later with two cups. When he stepped into the cabin Captain Newton pointed out toward the direction they were traveling. "Looks like a school of dolphin out there."

Caleb stepped to the side window and looked out and down to see twenty or so dolphins frolicking in the bow waves.

"Well?"

Caleb turned to the captain. "Well, what?"

"What are they saying?" Captain Newton asked with a smile. "You understood that parrot, didn't you?"

"I'm not sure that's what happened."

The captain waved him away. "Go down there and see if they have any news for me."

"Ah, okay."

Caleb left the cabin and went down to stand at the rail on the lowest deck. He stood there a minute, then shrugging, yelled, "Do you fish have any news for the captain?"

A moment later, a snout stuck out of the water. "Who are you?" a dolphin asked.

"Well, I'll be..." Caleb grinned and began a very strange conversation.

CHAPTER EIGHT

"Anna, come play." A ten-year-old girl waved, turned around, and ran across the wide, green park to the other children there.

Anna sat on a moss covered stone bench under a juniper tree, her legs crossed at the knees. Vines tangled their way up and down the trunk and branches and hung, drooping like sagging fuzzy ropes on an old sailing ship. Clouds skated across a blue sky. Trees grew everywhere, a hundred shades of green with every other color dashed among the branches.

Oscar and Helen, close friends, sat beside her watching the children toss a ball across the grass. Dogs barked in the distance. A large bear ambled across the park a hundred feet away followed by three dogs, a fox, and a large cat. A squirrel rode on the bear's back. Anna could hear the chittering from where she sat. The children laughed and danced around the wild park.

"Evidently they think of me as a child," Anna said.

"At heart, surely," Oscar said.

"I like watching the children. Doesn't mean I like playing their games. I'm over a thousand years old, after all."

Helen changed the subject. "Have any more dreams?"

"Yeah, every night. I'm not sure what to make of them. Last night I dreamed of Caleb."

"That's not new," Helen said.

"Yeah, but in this dream, he was riding a warhorse, wearing shiny armor and sword and all that. He looked fierce. It was a little scary at first."

"What happened?" Oscar asked. "Tell us from the beginning."

"Oh, you know how strange dreams are."

"The strange stuff is the best part."

"Okay," Anna sighed. "If you get bored, don't blame me... I'm walking through the field by the stream at the old mill outside our village. The sun is bright. Everything is nice, as usual, when a cold breeze whips up and dark clouds gather from out of nowhere. I hear a crack of lightning, I think. And moaning and yelling. Very sad, except I don't get sad; I get angry. You know me. How often have you seen me angry? Never, right? So, I'm angry at something when a man rides across the field out of white fog carrying a sword, dressed up in all that armor. Somehow, I know it's Caleb. He announces he will slay the dragon of injustice and bring peace to the land."

Oscar said, "Okay, now that sounds familiar."

"You haven't been reading books about chivalry and all that, have you?" Helen asked.

Anna frowned. "You know I don't read that stuff. This was right out of ...actually, I just don't know."

"I know what it means. It means you miss Caleb," Oscar said.

"I do miss him, but I know when the time is right, he'll be reborn here as I have. He'll find me. I'm patient. We all are—if we're listening to the Spirit at all."

Oscar rose to his feet. "I have an announcement to make."

"Oh?" Helen said.

"Yeah, I've been thinking about it for a long time. You know how I am. Don't want to rush into things, especially important things."

"So, get to the announcement, will you?" Anna urged.

"Oh yeah, ah, uh, I'm going to the tower."

Helen smiled. "I'm not surprised, Oscar. You've been talking about doing it for at least two years."

Anna leaned against the cool stone at her back, thoughtful, while Helen and Oscar talked about the coming trip. They all knew how far away the tower was. From their small village near the western wall in what was still considered to be Greece, the trip would be almost three-hundred miles east across Turkey, then south another six-hundred fifty toward Israel where the tower stood, sitting astride the country of Israel. It rose fifteen hundred miles, even above the clouds. The single entrance was always open to the garden.

"So, you've finally decided to go," Anna said. "Are you taking the train or going by river or what?"

"Oh, no. I'm strictly traditional. I'll be walking. It'll give me more time to think about my readiness."

"I know what you mean," Helen said. "I know a guy who lived at the university by the entrance. He said a lot of people who have gone to the tower, even most of the professors there, have never gone inside. They would sit at the entrance, sometimes for days, then decide they weren't quite ready for that amount of truth. There is a phrase they use: Being born is only in only one direction. Or something like that. Anyway, I'm sure you'll do fine. They say you can leave the tower anytime you want or travel upward if you want to."

"I'll take my time, get familiar with the garden first. That'll probably take years, then I'll consider going up to the next floor."

"I've heard there are seven hundred levels. I knew a really great guy who went to level three, once," Helen said.

"I met a guy once who went to level five and lived there for a while but went back to level three. He said he thought he was ready, but realized he just wasn't," Oscar said.

"We all know someone," Helen said. "It's good to know we have all the time we need."

Anna sighed, "I need to go somewhere and think." She stood and hugged her two friends. "Congratulations, Oscar, I'll be praying for you," then she walked away in the direction of the stream that ran through the valley toward the Aegean lakes.

A few hours later, Anna walked along the stream, stopping occasionally to dip her bare feet in the cool water. Her dreams were really beginning to occupy much of her thoughts lately. She stopped at a long fallen tree and sat, quietly watching the stream flow slowly by. A bird landed on the log a few feet away, looking for a snack, then a few more landed and began chirping and squabbling. A few minutes later a mama rabbit and babies crawled from under the log and looked up at her with soulful eyes.

"Are you all going to start begging?" Anna asked gently.

She heard the high-pitched hum of a craft passing by overhead and knew it was from the tower.

The tower was always a presence in the minds of all the citizens of New Jerusalem. She knew the tower dwellers traveled back and forth to parts unknown, sometimes in the flying craft. She always smiled at the sight. She was from the time of ancient Rome, Carthage to be exact. Such craft had been unknown in her first life.

The sound of the craft's mysterious mechanism changed, telling Anna it was slowing and getting closer. She stood and shaded her eyes as a spherical craft the size of a large truck appeared high above the trees and descended through the branches to hang suspended a few inches from the ground fifty feet away in the clearing.

The front irised open and a messenger stepped out.

"Greetings, Anna Hudson." The messenger bowed.

Anna bowed in return. "Honor to you, Messenger," she said, eyes wide.

"Honor to our Lord," he returned.

Anna nervously asked." How may I be of service, Messenger?"

"Anna Hudson, I come from our High King and Lord. You are summoned to the throne," he said.

Anna put her hand to her mouth and stepped back. She turned to look for support from her friends, but they were not there. "I...could there be a mistake? I am not one to..."

"There is no mistake, Anna. All will be well. Do not fear." He leaned forward and smiled. "I have been in His presence and am I not well?"

"You seem to be, sir, but you are..."

"... merely your servant," he said, bowing his head.

"What is this about, if I may ask?"

"You may certainly ask, Anna. I can tell you that Caleb is nearing the city and on his way to the tower. He has also been called. Other than that, it is my master's will to fill you in on further details in person."

When the messenger said 'in person' Anna felt faint. To be in his presence was something she never thought would happen. Never desired, never was ready to accept the reality of it. And Caleb? Caleb is finally here, and he arrives under these circumstances? Both elated and anxious, Anna stepped back and sat on the log.

The messenger put out a hand to steady her. "All will be well, Anna. You have been chosen. Our Lord sees you as his daughter. He knows your heart. He wishes you well. You are free to decline, and he will find someone else, but you are the best person for his plan."

"What is this plan?" she asked.

"I do not know the details of his plan for you. All I know is it is a plan you would willingly make your own."

Anna stood back up, shaking off her doubts. "I will not decline. I accept and will... Will you be taking me in that?" She pointed to the shiny silver craft.

The messenger smiled. "No, Anna. You will need time to prepare yourself. I suggest you take your time and walk. It will be a pleasant journey."

A minute later, Anna watched the craft rise into the air and thought about how she would explain this to Oscar and Helen.

"There is no way I'm staying here," Helen said.

Anna took her hand. "Good. Because I'm really nervous about this."

"We'll travel together," Oscar said. "It'll be great. We can tell each other stories along the way."

The next morning Oscar, Helen, and Anna stood on the dirt road at the edge of their village. Most of the villagers were there to see them off. She had dressed in breeches and walking boots, a wide brimmed hat, and a sleeveless jacket with lots of pockets. She had a small backpack slung over her shoulder.

Oscar shouted, "Wish us well. Pray for our journey."

The villagers shouted back waving their arms. Children ran up to them and hugged them.

Anna nodded to her friends, then stepped out onto the dirt road and started down the hill to the east.

The wall before them loomed high and grey as the *Mercy* floated in the bobbing water, standing off five-hundred feet. They had approached a little from the north and turned south for a few miles to get to the middle western gates. It was late and the light was dimming. Huge letters in the Hebrew language dominated the lower fifty feet of the wall. As they approached closer to the gate, they saw lights of the town reflecting off it. The town had, slowly over the centuries, grown closer and closer to the gate, even to the point of perching on stilts much like ancient Venice before it was destroyed. Now it hugged the wall for almost twenty miles, twelve of those out into the shallow water of the greater Mediterranean Lake.

Captain Newton pointed to the round entrance, the white circle of the gate, itself, sitting against the wall leaving the entrance open for all who would enter. He yelled, "Glorious, isn't it?"

They all stood on the upper deck, the captain directly above them and pointing.

"What a sight," Caleb said.

"I don't know why I waited so long to come here," Gelder said wistfully.

Chen leaned against the bannister. "We all know. It's all about being ready."

"So true." Jake stood with his back to a bulkhead wall moving slightly with the roll of the boat. As they got closer, they came close to other boats coming and going. The riverboat rolled with the converging wash from other passing vessels moving slowly, most under lowered sail. A sailing clipper passed them with sails down and a wisp of steam rising from a single thin stack.

Someone had resurrected an old two-stack steamship from a surviving museum or made it from scratch. It sat against the dock unloading passengers and cargo. The world seemed to be slowly gaining back its old technology.

Captain Newton yelled down to his passengers, "In a hundred years or two we'll see most of the sailing ships berthed and more steamers out on the water. In a thousand years it will all be electric if the Lord allows, or something arcane and wondrous."

They entered the line forming as ships finished their affairs and departed, leaving open berths. The sun was brightening the sky as they slid up to the dock. The *Mercy* threw out ropes and a crewman jumped to the dock and tied off.

The town started about a hundred yards from the docks. A wide boulevard marked the way to the gate running through the town and curving away to disappear around a curve in the road hidden by low buildings. The gate itself and the wall of the great city were only three hundred yards away.

Captain Newton ordered the plank slid out and was the first to disembark, followed by a few crewmen, then Julia, Caleb, Jake, and the others. They congregated at the foot of the ramp, then made their way across the port to an open cafe and sat down to discuss logistics.

Julia waved toward the town center. "Captain, how long will we be here?"

"I'm not sure. I'll need to talk to the port master. They'll let us stay here at least a day, I'm assuming."

"Well, I would like to take Tam around the town and see what's what," Julia said.

Me, too, " Jake said. "Then I intend to walk through that gate and see what's on the other side."

The captain turned to Caleb. "Well. You're the main reason we're here. It's either this gate or the one in Greece."

Caleb looked up at the looming wall. "It seems to me I'll be at least three hundred miles closer to the tower from here. So, I'll be getting off here and going straight east."

"Me, too," Chen said.

"So, three of you are getting off here." He turned to Julia. "And you?"

"I think I'll be closer to Mom in Greece." She hugged Tam to her. "Tam's with me. We'll travel to the tower from there."

"Okay, then. I need to talk to a man. Meet you all here at sundown?" The captain looked at them all. "Let's meet here and say our farewells, at least for the present time, okay?"

They all nodded.

"Good. Go have fun. See you all in, say, ten hours?"

After receiving a chorus of agreement, the captain stood and walked away toward the port master's office.

The journey from her small village started a new phase in Anna's life. Though she could hardly get Caleb off her mind, any time she thought about her coming *actual*-meeting-with-Jesus, the ruler of the entire world, her feet slowed to a stop, and she stood in a daze till one of her friends patted her on the back and reassured her how it would all work out. Their first day ended in a town called Kavalla where they spent the night.

The next day they entered Alexandropoulos, once a port city, now a happy village of farmers and fishermen and craftsmen, but now two miles from the Aegean. They rounded a sharp bend and came upon another traveler sitting in the shade of a broad tree just off the road.

"Evening, friend," called Oscar.

The traveler stood as they approached. "Evening fellow travelers. You seem tired. Come to my fire. I have enough food for all."

As they approached, Anna saw four bowls set out. Stew steamed in each and dark rough bread sat on a board by each bowl.

Blankets were already spread out on the ground. They all sat and waited for their benefactor to explain.

"You were expecting us? Helen asked.

"Yes. When our Lord calls, we make the way easy."

"Ah..., so you are a messenger, then," Anna said.

"I'm what you would call a companion," he said, smiling at them all. He turned his gaze on Anna. "I know you quite well, Anna. I was there and watched when your mother gave you to the world."

Anna's eyes went wide. "You were there? The whole time? While I grew up?"

"Yes, Anna. I was your guardian till you left the first world, then with my task complete I came to this city." He pointed up to the sky. "Back then it was way up there."

Anna covered her face, overcome. When she pulled her hands back, tears streamed down her face. She leaned close to the angel, took his hand, and kissed it. "Thank you for protecting me."

The angel put his hand on her head and said, "Blessed be the Lord God Almighty, maker of heaven and earth, who gives life to us all. I accept your thanks, Anna. It is my joy to do so as it is His joy to give you peace."

"What is your name, if I may ask?" Helen said.

"My name is Sandon." He bowed from the waist, still sitting.

Having recovered from a brief moment of shock, Anna asked, "Why are you here? Are we in danger?"

Sandon laughed heartily. "No, no danger. I am to guide you if you want me to."

Oscar laughed. "I'm scared half to death of going anywhere close to the tower. I've heard of its power to cut to the soul."

"Well said, Oscar. That is why I'm here. To advise if you wish to listen."

"I feel a little relieved already. Are there more guides like you at the tower?" Oscar said.

"Yes, millions."

"Will you go all the way with us?" Helen asked.

"No," Sandon shook his head. "I will go only so far as Eden's garden. There you will meet the keepers. They will show you to the river's origin and refreshment and will prepare you. There will be much to do. You will need to be very patient and listen carefully to them."

"That makes me even more nervous," Anna said.

Sandon smiled kindly. "You'll have many good memories of those moments. Just wait till you see Life's tree. It is so big you cannot see all of it even from a half mile away. And wait till you taste its fruit. Nothing is so good."

"Wow." Helen breathed.

"It's been here the whole time I've been on the new Earth, and I've been putting off going. Why did I do that?" Oscar said, half to himself.

"The tree is nourished by this world and nourishes us in kind. It is available, but only to those who wish it strongly enough." Sandon spoke carefully as he looked around at them.

"Strongly enough for what?" Anna asked. "Wait, I think I already know the answer."

"Yes, you do. Shall I say it?" He waited.

Anna paused a moment, then nodded.

"The moment of truth is when you stand at the entrance of the tower. Do you go in or turn away? Another moment is when you gaze upon the tree. Do you accept its fruit or pull your hand away? There are many such moments on one's way upward in the tower. Even my fellow brothers have traveled this road. Some further than others.

"The issue is, do you want life enough to take it because even here in this perfect place, you still are less than our Lord and Our Creator God. If you wish to become more than you are, you must give some of yourself away."

"That's what I thought it would be," Anna said.

Sandon spread his palm flat on his chest. "The answer is to love yourself a little less and accept His answer as to who you were made to be."

"Sounds really hard," Oscar said.

Sandon nodded. "For some. Others find it easy at times, but usually after a lifetime of trying. Many are far from being that person and the journey for them will be difficult."

"This is deep, scary stuff," Anna said.

Sandon nodded. "Rightly so. Let's change the subject. Ah..., shall I tell you the history of the world? Ask me anything you like."

The conversation became light and filled with gasps of surprise and annoyance. They talked deep into the night and woke the next morning to a fresh day.

CHAPTER FOUR

L ily Primrose yawned as she rose from the straw pallet she used for a bed in her small cabin. Stretching, she looked through her glassless window and, with delight, saw her cow standing by the stall and chickens gathering for their morning feeding. "Oh, another wonderful day."

She hummed to herself as she ambled outside to find the chickens staring at the ground scratching for feed not yet thrown out. The brown heifer nuzzled her hair leaving drops of slobber.

"Ew, Elly, I told you to wipe your mouth after you drink. Now I'll need to wash my hair again. Oh, well, no problem."

She hugged the cow and asked, "Are you going to give me some milk today? You know the chickens said I could have eggs. And I'll get some honey and put a little in your grain. How's that for a deal?"

The cow nodded her head and turned to the barn where a small calf waited. A milk pail hung on a peg driven into the wall.

"Alrighty then. You're such a nice cow. I'll feed the chickens first, then we can get some milk and fix breakfast."

An hour later, Lily sat at the table in the small cottage at the edge of the forest having had breakfast, and sang softly to herself. Only one thing diminished the wonder of the day. Even after all these years she still missed the dog she'd had as a child. Her white, fuzzy chihuahua had often protected her from reaching hands and pasty smiles, once, even, from another dog and came away with half an ear gone. Lily's song faded for a moment as she touched her own ear and thought about her poor little friend. Soon her smile returned as she put the dishes away and straightened the covers on her bed.

Outside the sun rose higher in the sky promising a warm day—a good day to be out in the garden tending to her greens and tomatoes and all the other veggies the neighbors in the nearby hamlet loved to eat.

There was something about Lily that made folks wonder. She had lived in the same cottage for well over a hundred years, even before Dave Gallagher moved in close by and the Johnsons moved in later, then the M'tumbes after that. She always smiled when they came by to get veggies and heap praise on her animals. But she had never asked anyone over nor left the confines of her little patch of heaven except to get water from the stream.

Dave Gallagher once suggested she go with him to the village fair held every spring, but the look of fear on her face quelled the idea. He relented, but he still had a special place in his heart for her.

With breakfast finished, Lily placed her dishes in a basket and started down the well-worn path she had walked many times to the spring-fed stream nearby. It was a path used by Dave as well.

This morning Dave sat on his back porch and watched her walk by. When he waved, she waved back with a smile.

"It's a good morning to be sure, Ms. Lily," he called.

She called back, "So it is, Mr. Gallagher. So, it is."

She walked with a little more spunk than usual. She felt a little more free than usual, too. As she approached the spring, he watched from his porch like he'd done before. As she hunkered down to wash the dishes, a bird landed on her shoulder. Startled, she lost her footing and fell face-first in the waist-deep stream.

Alarmed, Dave jumped up from his chair and ran down the path to the water's edge. "Ms. Lily?"

She stood in the water sputtering, then lapsed into silent shock as a vision from her past flitted through her consciousness.

"Ms. Lily?" he called.

She stared in space, horror in her eyes.

He waded into the stream and approached her. She didn't see him, only her vision.

He touched her shoulder.

She screamed and looked around wildly, and seeing him, grabbed him around the waist and clung fiercely.

He slowly put his arms around her. Standing in the stream, Lily let a person touch her for the first time since her childhood. Of course, Dave knew nothing of this, but he did know during the first twenty years in this valley Lily never spoke a word except to her animals. It was another ten years before she would even acknowledge his presence. He recognized trauma, and he recognized a person in need, and he reckoned that heaven was just such a place as this—a place to heal.

CHAPTER TEN

The passage through the gate into the great city went without incident. It was plenty wide enough for a large group to pass through at the same time. Everyone seemed to sense the importance of the moment and passed through quietly. After passing the inner threshold, many mentioned a feeling of warmth and comfort passing through them.

Caleb, Jake, and Chen paused and stared out at water as far as the eastern horizon.

"I kinda supposed we were finished with the lakes, but it seems the wall just cut straight through the Mediterranean leaving water on both sides," Jake said.

A port had been built on the other side of the gate and a village had grown up around it.

"So, do we take another boat or walk?" Chen pointed south where they could see the town curving to the east following the shoreline stretching into the distance.

Caleb hitched his pack higher on his shoulder. "I don't know about you guys, but I'm a little tired of sitting on a boat. I say we walk the rest of the way. It's only seven-hundred miles. Maybe we can hitch a ride on a passing truck or something. I wish I knew what the time schedule was. I'd know what kind of hurry we should be in."

"Should be another village within a few days' walk." Jake sidled over to a street-side stall selling trinkets and asked about the road going east. He came back. "Right. Three days walk and a fishing village. If we stay to the old coastal road, we'll see it easy enough."

Chen shrugged. "Let's start. I'm in the mood for walking." They adjusted their packs and started out and in a few hours were well outside the village by the wall. The ocean was to their north and warm dry air from the African plain to the south dried the sweat from their faces. By the time the sun set behind them, they found a secluded nook among the rocks and sand of the beach, built a fire, and prepared a bit of dried fish, cheese and bread they'd bought earlier.

Chen sat facing the fire with legs crossed. "I like this life. To me, this is the heaven I conceived of in my first life. To travel, meet new people, see new things. I've always been a person who wanted to move."

"Know the feeling well," Jake said, reaching for a piece of driftwood and stirring the fire.

Caleb said, "It's what I did for the last fifteen years of my life before the mortar fell and ended that."

"You were a military leader, right?" Chen asked.

Caleb nodded his head.

"You had many men who answered to you?"

"Yeah, I had two hundred men under my direct command. I saw them every day," Caleb said.

"At the time I died," Chen said, "I had twenty who answered to me. You had many. Perhaps you are a Daimyo. I don't know. The western way was confusing."

Caleb held up a hand. "I was a captain in the army with two-hundred men under me. The next rank was colonel, who commanded as much as four captains, or around a thousand men. Then it just keeps going up with more men."

"It is confusing; it changes every generation. It gets confusing without even trying," Jake said.

"Did you use the sword?" Chen asked Caleb.

"No, we had guns and bombs. Most of my men carried a ten-inch knife on their side. I carried a pistol and long gun, usually. And a few grenades for fun."

Jake said, "We used swords, but not very often, usually just stand in line, load your musket and try not to get hit by a lead ball."

"I see. But that is not a warrior's way," Chen said.

"Right," Caleb stared into the fire. "We weren't warriors. We were soldiers. Big difference. We had to learn to work together. Everyone had his specialty. I gave the orders and my lieutenant passed them to the sergeants, who figured out how to get it done. Simple enough."

"Yeah, then you still tried not to get hit by a lead ball or a big iron four-pounder," Jake said.

"Yeah." Caleb threw another piece of driftwood on the fire. "That much had not changed. You'd still pick a target, take him out and try not to get hit. The last three years I was a little more free to make my own rules, though. I resigned from the Army and joined a private outfit. I personally picked most of my men."

"As a samurai, one was required to see the other's eyes. I knew, well, the man who killed me. He grew up in the next village. His name was Yuito, a good man. He killed me, as was his duty. I hope he made it here."

Caleb said, "A soldier's duty can be a hard one. If you're signed up with the right side, the decision to fire or not becomes a little easier, but not much."

Chen asked, "Your master, was he a good man?"

"You mean when I went to the private sector? Yeah, I think so. General Mathis, retired, was a hard man, but fair and valued the men under his command. He only sent us out on missions that supported the right side. I never needed to worry about that. A few times it was helping take down a tin-pot dictator. Usually, though, it was helping refugees or a small government with neighbor problems."

Jake motioned up to the white haze high in the eastern sky. "What do you suppose the Lord wants you for?"

"I truly have no idea. I can't imagine how my military experience could add anything, at all, to the capabilities those angels have. I just need to wait... Maybe he needs someone to sweep the floor. I could do that."

"Well, it'll be a long walk tomorrow. I'm going to sleep." Jake leaned back on the blanket he'd laid on the sand and closed his eyes.

"Oyasumi Nasai," Chen said and did the same.

Caleb leaned back on his mat by the fire and thought of his upcoming meeting. He couldn't shake the feeling that he had a huge learning curve to climb. This was heaven, for crying out loud.

Remembering an incident in his childhood, he thought, Mom must have prayed for me a lot. Maybe I'd made that crucial decision as a kid. "Jesus is Lord", she would say. She must have told me a thousand times. It must have sunk in because here I am sitting by a fire on the beach instead of in a fire in...who-knows-where --the bad place.

The night wore on, he closed his eyes and slept a fitful sleep.

The next morning, they roused with the rising sun. Caleb woke with a hand on his shoulder. He looked up to see Chen with a concerned look on his face. Chen tilted his head to the east and Caleb sat up and stared.

In the distance, a man was walking along the beach. It was obvious to a trained eye the stranger was a warrior. He carried a staff or gun or something on his side.

Caleb reached over and shook a snoring Jake, who jumped and looked around.

"What?" Jake followed Caleb's thumb and saw the figure approaching them. He was closer now and it was clear he was fitted in light armor and carried a sword at his side. A round shield was slung over his shoulder.

They stood and faced him as the stranger approached and stopped fifty feet away.

"Hello, friend," Caleb said, spreading his arms wide.

The stranger remained silent for a moment. Caleb studied him. He was perhaps a head taller than Caleb, who was not a small man. He wore a dark helmet. His eyes seemed serious enough.

The warrior said, "Are one of you Caleb Carson?"

"I am," Caleb said.

"You are to turn around and return to your village," the stranger said.

Caleb's eyes went wide. This was the last thing he expected. He thought he was getting an escort, but not out of town.

"Who are you?" Jake demanded.

"I am not important," the stranger said. "You are a warrior. You are not allowed in the holy city."

Caleb kept his hands apart, palms visible. "There must be a mistake. I've been summoned. An angel showed up and said so. Contact your superiors; they'll tell you."

"I know of no mistake. This is my area of responsibility. You must leave or I will remove you and your men." He rested his hand on the hilt of his sword.

"Hold on now." Caleb stepped back and glanced sideways to see Chen, to his left, step three paces away and two paces forward. Jake, on his right, placed himself near a pile of driftwood they'd gathered. This was happening way too fast. Who was this guy?

Caleb, face grim, held his hands up higher. "Hold on, partner. You need to contact your boss and find out what's what. You need to check in. Get on your radio or whatever and check in. You're mistaken. I've been called."

"I know of no mistake. You have been warned." The warrior pulled his helmet off and let it drop to the sand revealing short-cut blonde hair and hazel eyes, slowly pulled his sword and began walking to the three men.

Oh crap, Caleb thought, What is this guy's problem? He glanced quickly to both sides. Jake had thrown a long piece of driftwood to Chen, who was testing the heft of it and was picking another up for himself.

The stranger saw Jake pick up the driftwood and paused to slip the shield from his shoulder.

Caleb stood facing the stranger, hands empty. Then he snatched up his blanket, rolled it around his left arm, and took a piece of wood Jake handed him.

Chen stepped forward. "Stranger?" he called. The warrior turned to him.

"What is your name?" Chen called. The warrior remained silent.

"So be it." Chen charged, completely catching the warrior off guard. Chen reached him in three quick strides, went to a knee, and swept his length of wood to crack against the stranger's elbow. The sword flew away to land on the sand.

Jake charged. The stranger deflected Jake's charge with a quick swipe of his shield, then shifting his weight, slammed the flat of it against Chen's head, knocking him to the ground.

Caleb was right behind Jake and as the warrior turned back to face Caleb, Caleb slammed him to the ground, losing his club and blanket. Then making a fist, began pounding the stranger anywhere there was no armor.

He got two good hits on the warrior's chin before the tide turned and with a heft, Caleb went flying backward.

As Caleb scrambled to rise, Chen was already staggering to his feet, dazed, but shaking it off quickly. Jake was now behind the warrior and rising.

The warrior stood for a second and spying the sword lunged for it, but Caleb rolled over, shielding it from him. The same time Chen swept the warrior from his feet and both he and Jake piled on and tried desperately to pin the warrior down.

Lying in the sand, Caleb grabbed the warrior around the neck. "What, the heck, is your problem?" he gasped near the warrior's ear. The warrior smashed an elbow against Caleb's face, pushed both of the others off him, and pulled the sword from the sand. Then with a quick surge rose to a knee and plunged the sword through Chen's chest and with a quick reverse did the same to Jake.

Caleb's heart went cold. The warrior rose to his feet and lifted the sword over Caleb's head. Stunned, Caleb whispered," Lord, what do I do?"

As the words left Caleb's lips, the warrior said, "About time, Warrior Caleb," and disappeared in a flash of stars.

A few minutes passed as Caleb sat on the sand and stared at the place the stranger had been standing. The sparkles dissipating in the air told him this was not any warrior, but another angel like the messenger that brought him news of his calling back in Savannah. He looked at his two friends lying still, blood staining the sand red.

Then, with a groan, Chen said, "Ow, that hurt," as he opened his eyes and looked around. A few seconds later, Jake rolled over on an elbow. "Damn, I didn't like that."

Chen pulled his shirt up and wiped blood from a completely healed wound. "Wow, that was fast." He looked up at Caleb.

Caleb sat across the sand, still stunned, but now wiping tears from his eyes. "You guys okay?" he asked.

"Yeah. Now I am." Jake muttered.

Chen raised himself to his knees. "What was that about?"

"Yeah, good question. Let's try to avoid doing that again," Jake said.

"It was all about teaching me a lesson and I think you guys took the brunt of it," Caleb said, voice still shaky from adrenalin.

"What lesson?" Jake asked.

Caleb pointed at the sandal prints in the sand. "That was no mere warrior. That was another angel. If I had asked the Lord what to do as soon as he told us to leave, he would have disappeared then, not after he stabbed you two."

"Oh," Jake said.

Recovering, Caleb stood, pulled his friends up from the sand, and patted them on the shoulder. "You guys okay to travel?"

Jake shrugged. "I feel okay. The pain is gone, though the memory is still there."

"By the way, that was a good move, knocking the sword out of his hand like that," Caleb said, brushing sand off Chen's back.

"It worked, but he was very strong," Chen said.

"He flung us around like rag dolls," Jake complained, as he checked his own wounds. He pointed across the sand." Hey, Boss, look over there. The sword and shield lay in the sand twenty feet away.

Chen walked over and picked up the sword. "This is heavy. I couldn't use it very well."

Jake picked up the shield, put his arms through the straps, and tested the unusual feel of a fighting tool he'd never been trained to use. "Maybe we're supposed to get used to using them. Doesn't make any sense to me. We're not angels and there aren't any bad guys to deal with. It's a mystery."

Right now, Caleb wanted nothing to do with the weapons that had slain his friends. "Let's wrap them in a bedroll and take them with us. Don't want them lying around. I think it's time to move on. He might come back."

A few minutes later they resumed their journey east to the tower of light.

CHAPTER ELEVEN

"Did you dream well?" Sandon asked, sitting cross legged by the warm ashes of their fire.

Anna opened her eyes and looked around. "How did you know I was dreaming?"

"Your eyes were moving under your lids," Helen said, sitting up with a blanket wrapped around her shoulders against the morning chill.

"Good morning to all." Oscar approached the camp. "I went up the hill to check out the view."

Helen said, "And?"

"The town is to the southeast about a half-hour walk. To the west is open country. I saw a herd of cows out there. South is the road to Bursa and east is more of the same green hills."

Ten minutes later they were up and traveling the well-worn dirt road. None were hungry yet, so they walked and chatted. The weather was a little cool still but would be warm in another hour. The road constantly curved and bent to accommodate erosion and rocks protruding from the hillside. Clouds accented the blue sky letting streamers of sunlight pass through which added to the light from the tower six-hundred miles away.

Presently, they came upon the valley where the town of Dilovaci sat. Smoke rose from the chimneys of grey stone cottages.

Anna, walking beside Sandon, asked, "Do you suppose this town looked like this before the great war?"

"No. This is almost all rebuilt since then." As he walked, he glanced toward Anna. "I was in that war. Almost all the angels participated. This part of the world was hit harder than most."

Oscar said from Sandon's other side, "I often thought about that war. Why did this area get hit harder?"

Sandon raised his arm and pointed east, south, and west. "For a thousand miles in these three directions we're the places most in need of cleansing. To the south Satan's throne was located in Pergamos on Cypress." Sandon lifted a hand and waved toward the south. "I saw the fire fall from heaven and lay waste to the entire island. To the west, the city of the harlot received the same fate. Babylon, Arabia, most of Palestine were totally wiped clean. Jerusalem and the place of our Lord's birth were preserved. Now, New Jerusalem sits upon the land and the center of the tower sits astride the old Jerusalem. When you enter Eden, you can see it there--a small town in the middle of a garden forty miles wide by forty miles long."

The dirt road ended when they entered the town. Like the homes, the street leading through the town was paved in stone. Still being early morning, the townspeople were yet rising. Merchants, though, were already up and shutters to shops were open. A few people sat outside drinking their morning beverage and having breakfast. The smell of bread wafted down the street to them on a light breeze.

"That smells good," Helen said.

"Yeah, let's stop here. We can travel better with a full stomach." Oscar turned to the others.

"Sure. We have time." Sandon waved them towards the bakery and cafe a few blocks away.

They entered the cafe, stepping into a dim interior large enough for twenty people. Wooden benches lined the walls with round tables and chairs set strategically around the room. A few folk lounged and talked.

Heads turned when they entered, and several people smiled a welcome.

The proprietor, who was also the baker, came out of a side room. "Welcome friends. We have fresh bread and butter. Also, porridge with honey and cheeses and pancakes."

"Don't forget coffee," one of the patrons said at the baker's back.

He hooked a thumb behind him. "Jonah is right. We have good coffee."

As they settled into chairs, Anna asked, "Sandon, what did you mean we have time? Are we on a schedule?"

Sandon shrugged. "Not really. It depends on you. Will you want to visit your parents before your meeting? Or visit a few places of interest? Or maybe you'd like to meet with Caleb before the meeting. He is also on his way there."

"That's easy. Let's find Caleb first, I've been waiting a long time for him to get here."

"Of course."

The baker came back with a flat board a foot long with a handle carved into it. A loaf of fresh bread sat atop it with a small bowl of soft, white butter. They all gave him their breakfast orders.

"Anna said, "You said Caleb is on his way. When will he get to the tower?"

"That depends on him. I don't know right now. He has been tested and there is more to come. But I have confidence in those our Lord chooses. He knows Caleb's heart. Caleb will prevail; he will overcome."

"What about me?" Anna said.

"Oh? What about you?" Sandon asked.

"Will I overcome?" Anna asked. "I'm not so sure."

Sandon swept his gaze around the table. "Many have not overcome, yet. Many righteous citizens of New Jerusalem live outside the tower's entrance. Some of them are waiting for the right time to step forward. Some are still afraid to give away what they don't need—cherished ideas of themselves. Many are still afraid of what they will become. They are still infants, though many have gained much knowledge. The university there is always full of students who feel the need for further preparation. They don't realize they will know all they need to know once they enter in."

Sandon used the knife lying on the table to cut a thick slice of bread and buttered it. "You could think of it as healing. Our beliefs are what holds us together. When someone loses a cherished belief, something must replace it. That should be our Lord's truth.

"Strive to lose all beliefs you have that are not totally true; learn to easily let them go. You think you do well, but your efforts, though necessary, are yet still minor. It's far better to trust Him; you have a long way to go.

"But don't worry. Learn to enjoy the journey. The tower is high, even to the heavens beyond and out into God's universe. It only gets better the farther you go. I have seen it, though even I have not seen it all—not even close."

"I didn't realize the tower went out there," Helen said, in awe.

Sandon nodded, then turned to Anna. "Does that answer your question?"

She mumbled, "I suppose so," and grabbed a piece of bread. "Actually, no it doesn't." She took a bite and thought about Caleb, wondering what he was doing.

The sun was just rising when Abdul gave up on catching more fish and pulled the net from the water. The twenty-foot wooden boat yawed ten degrees as he pulled the net back into the boat to land at the bottom, covering the fifty-or-so large fish he'd spent the night catching. He liked fishing at night. He liked the cool air and the stars above. The waters west of Alexandria always gave him his night's catch.

He enjoyed thinking about important things while working his mundane job, like what the stars were there for and if they had names. Sometime, on restful nights, he'd lie on the bottom of the boat, drifting with the waves. Staring up at the stars for hours, he'd pretend they were old friends. There was Amun and Sara, Anippe and Panya. For Abdul, naming them made them real. He needed friends on lonely nights, miles out in the Mediterranean. Back on shore he'd sell his catch, get a few hours of sleep, and spend the rest of his time working on his boat and repairing the shack he'd found on the beach.

As the morning current brought him closer to the shore, he saw the three men walking along the beach headed east. Soon they'd be passing by his home. He pulled out his oars and helped the old boat catch the waves and left the strangers behind as he hurried to the shore and his home.

By the time he had unloaded the boat and stashed his cargo behind the shack, the three strangers were visible coming toward him down the beach on the line between dry sand and wet. He sat in the doorway of his home and waited for them to pass.

As they got even with his line of sight, they stopped and approached.

"Morning, friend," one of them said.

"Morning, stranger."

"I'm Jake. This is Chen and Caleb. Can you tell us where we are in relation to the tower?"

Abdul studied them a moment. "Ten miles east is Alexandria. The tower is north from there, four day's walk."

Jake pulled his hat from his head. "You wouldn't happen to have drinking water, would you? We're a little low."

"I have only enough for me. Sorry."

"Ah, that's alright. Good day." Jake shrugged and returned to his companions, and they headed east to the town.

Abdul frowned as they walked away. He could have given them water. He had enough to share. He could always walk the ten minutes to his hidden stream and get more, but old habits die hard. And his short stay in this place had not yet taught him any new lessons. He remembered the incident that brought him here, although he had no real idea of where "here" was. The people at the nearby village gave him no trouble. Since his birth on this beach six years ago, he'd had no inclination to delve into the reason he woke one morning to find his life changed. He had walked down to the beach to find this shelter and the boat beached beside it. It was enough.

All he knew was the fishing was good. He was almost content with *only* that in this life, but sometimes the thought would intrude past the grey haze of his mundane existence that *other places* could reveal new purpose. Abdul wasn't ready for that. This was the life he wanted; this was the life he got—at least for now.

CHAPTER TWELVE

Captain Newton, Julia, Tam, and Gelder stood on the bottom deck and watched the *Mercy's* crew tie off to the dock. The Greek dockworkers finished in about two minutes and went about their other chores.

The trip north from the *middle-western* gate had been uneventful. After Caleb, Chen, and Jake passed through the middle gate on their way to the tower, Captain Newton settled affairs with the port authorities, then he and Gelder went exploring the town by the wall. They met later with Julia and Tam and, after an hour of checking cargo, cast off and headed to Greece and the *north*western gate.

"What are your plans?" Captain Newton asked Gelder.

"Same as yours. I plan on going into the city and finding out first-hand what I've heard for years: that the holy city is more than you can imagine. Well, I can imagine a lot, so I expect to be properly impressed."

"I think you will be."

Julia said, "I'm excited about finding Mom and maybe a lot of other relatives."

"You should be," Captain Newton told her. He pulled a small leather bag from a pocket and handed it to her. "You probably won't need this, but you shouldn't expect room and board for free, although it will usually be offered that way."

Julia opened the bag and found twenty small silver coins and a couple of gold ones. "Aw, thanks, Captain. That's very thoughtful. We can buy some gifts for Mom when we find her."

"Rightly so," he said. "And remember to go to the mayor's office first. They usually know where people live."

"I will." Julia paused and looked up and down the riverboat one last time. "It's been a privilege, Captain." She hugged him. Then Tam did the same. They gathered their packs and walked down the ramp and into the crowd on the dock.

"Nice girl," Gelder said, watching them walk away. "Now it's my time to say bye-for-now. Wish me good fortune." The ramp sagged a little as he walked down it and away into the crowd.

Captain Newton whispered, "Good fortune always, old friend." Then he turned to his crewmen and announced they would be here for at least a week. As the crew cheerfully started planning for shore leave, he retired to his cabin.

Julia and Tam were both excited to be out and about among total strangers. In all her years in heaven, Julia had met a few grumpy persons, but no bad people. Usually, encounters with strangers were a joy. More than once she had met a stranger who was a younger version of someone she knew in the old life or simply someone she'd heard of.

They had debarked at a port town called Preveza.

Over the next days, they traveled east through Greece, passing through Loutrakion, Petrona, then finally to Larisa, where the northernmost gate on the west wall was located. Larisa, like the town at the last stop, had grown right up to the gate. Like most of the cities and towns, Larisa had been almost totally destroyed by the conflagration that swept the world. The foundations of homes and other buildings had remained, however, and those souls who had once lived here had eventually moved back and began rebuilding.

Greece had grown wild in the intervening years and three-hundred year old forests grew in many places covering the mostly rocky terrain. Greece had been given a new start and the citizens were serious about making it more beautiful than ever. In spite of efforts to keep the atmosphere relaxed and slow, a tourist trade had grown up and travelers encountered many traders near the gate.

Julia, holding Tam's hand, walked among stalls selling or trading wares. It was fun. No pressure. The haggling was not in earnest as no one's living depended on making a profit. There was always food and shelter for those who had come upon difficult times. Those who were blessed with much were more than willing to help the needy.

Tam pulled Julia to a stop at a stall where a smiling girl of about ten greeted them.

"Hello, friends. Can I interest you in a balloon? My father makes them." She stepped aside to reveal shelves with miniature hot air balloons made from paper. "One places a candle in the bottom, and they rise up. You hold this string and watch it float in the breeze. They are especially beautiful at night."

Tam asked hopefully, "Can I see one?"

Julia, intrigued, said, "Sure, we're not in a hurry."

"Which one?" the girl asked. Tam pointed to the reddish translucent balloon shaped like a medieval castle.

She gingerly placed it on the counter between them. "What is your name?" she asked.

"Tam of Cyrene."

"I've not heard of Cyrene. Where is that?"

"On the south of..." Tam stammered. "In North Africa, on the coast."

"Is it by the gate there?"

"I don't think so," he said.

She asked, "Are you here to see the archives?"

Tam glanced up to Julia.

Julia asked, "What are the archives?"

"Oh, people leave their names and home locations at the archives near the gate in case someone wants to find them."

The archives were housed in a stone building fifty feet from the grey metal and stone wall and twenty feet off the road that led through the gate into the city.

Julia and Tam stopped outside the doorway to the building and looked up, searching for the top of the wall, but from the paved street, it rose over two-hundred feet and seemed to lean outward. Julia felt the imposing weight of it and had to remind herself of its solid construction. It wasn't built by man, but by angels and would last longer than Julia had the power to imagine.

They entered the cool interior to find a young man sitting at a desk.

He said, "Hello travelers. I'm assuming you are travelers; you have that look."

Julia said. "We're interested in seeing your list of names."

"Of course," he said and stood. "Follow me, please." He led them down a hallway with many doors. They entered the first door and went to a wide cabinet.

"We started collecting names almost a hundred-fifty years ago. The other gates were already doing it, so we were a little late getting started." The young man chatted as he opened a wide leather-bound ledger."

"You have a hundred-fifty years of names in this book?" Julia asked.

"Well, no ma'am. This is just my attempt at humor. This book only has about seven hundred names, the earliest. The names are really kept here." He opened a cabinet next to the desk to reveal a computer and screen. "I got this from a traveler many years ago and keep it running from parts I collect here and there. There is still a lot of old tech being dug up. I was a computer engineer in my past life."

Standing, he turned the computer on and asked," Name?"

"Dorothy Mathison," Julia said.

"Dorothy, Dorothy, ah yes, we have over a hundred Dorothy Mathisons. Place of birth?"

"London."

"Okay. Three. We have three names from there. One last week, it seems. Two others going back, oh seventy years."

"Where were they going? Does the machine show that?"

"Yes, the two older ones to Istanbul and Cypress, the one last week went to Armenia."

Julia stood over his shoulder and stared at the screen. "That doesn't help much, but I appreciate your help. I'll need to think about this new information."

"Can I try?" Tam asked.

"Sure, kid," the man said.

"Simon, of Cyrene," Tam said.

"Okay." The man typed the words in. "Alrighty. We got a message. 'To Tam. I am in Damascus with all the others.' He passed through a hundred twenty years ago."

Tam took Julia's hand as tears washed his eyes. "I want to go there. My granddad and my brothers will be there."

Julia knelt and gripped Tam's shoulders. "Sure, Tam. We'll go there. That will be our first priority."

They thanked the man and left the building.

As they walked through the wide round gate, Julia thought about all the people in this new, wonderful place who were traveling around looking for their loved ones. Even though she was very much looking forward to being with her mother, she knew she had all the time she needed. Her mother was happy and content wherever she was, and it was only a matter of time before they were united.

Julia looked up in wonder at the arch fifty feet above. When they exited the passage through the wall, Julia paused to scan a wide pavilion. She should have assumed there would be more towns on the other side. The street leading through the pavilion was paved with gold stones and led straight away past shops and open-air cafes. A woman approached them and handed them a bouquet of flowers and said, "Welcome to New Jerusalem."

Julia smiled, took the flowers, and smelled them. "Wow, I've never smelled anything like this." She held the flowers down for Tam to smell.

"I grow them outside town," the woman said. "Have a good stay." She turned away to offer flowers to a man walking past.

Julia and Tam continued down the cobblestone street. "Sweet smells and gold streets seem appropriate," Julia said to Tam. "I'm looking forward to what comes next."

They continued past the growing town and out into the countryside. In the near and far distance was evidence of farming and earthy industry. They passed a pasture of uncut hay. Further down the road, a herd of milk cows grazed lazily, tails swishing away non-existent gnats.

Later in the afternoon, they passed through a hamlet of four houses and a barn. Two men sat on barrels in the barn's doorway leaning back against the gray aged stone and wide rustic boards of the doorway.

"Good afternoon, travelers," An elderly white haired man raised a hand in greetings.

"The same to you, sir."

"Here, have a seat." He offered as he pointed to a couple of wicker chairs near at hand.

"Thanks." Julia led Tam to the chairs thinking it would be good to stop for a while and rest their feet and ignored Tam's impatient sigh.

"My name's Paul. This here's Woodruff."

"Julia and Tam."

A woman stepped out of a low built bungalow across the street and came over to them.

"It will be starting in an hour. Who are your new friends, Paul?" she asked.

"This is Julia and Tam. Julia, this is Charlotte."

Charlotte waved with a quick flourish. "You guys here for the party?"

Julia raised a brow. "What party?"

"We're having a shindig or hoedown or whatever they call it," Woodruff said.

"What's that? Sorry, I lived in England all my life before."

"It's like a party with dancing and singing and storytelling."

"Oh, it sounds nice." Tam seemed less in a hurry to move on.

"I never heard of one either till about two weeks ago. I was raised in Detroit," Woodruff said.

Paul patted him on the knee. "You'll like it, Woody. Just you wait and see. The girls will have you up and dancing in short order."

"That I will want to see," Charlotte said.

Julia looked down at Tam, noticing his eager expression. "Want to go to a party?"

The old barn appeared to be stout and solid. It reminded Julia of pictures she'd seen of new warehouses they were building when she was growing up in the 1800s outside of London. Inside, the squared timbers could easily be seen in the walls rising up twenty feet with clapboard siding attached to the outside. Across the top, timbers spanned forty feet or more and provided a hangout for pigeons and mice. The floor was swept dirt, packed solid with sprigs of hay.

The party was already in progress when they arrived. Neighbors from all around mingled and musicians played a lively country jig. Then a man with a guitar in hand joined them and danced around the makeshift stage and entertained listeners with a well-played rendition of a song Julia had never heard before. It was beautiful and was obviously played by a professional. The other musicians played along with him and smiled at his antics.

Against a far wall, a line of tables held an assortment of drinks, pastries, and other dishes.

"Help yourself," Charlotte said, taking Julia's elbow and walking her through the milling farmers. They made their way to the table and, seeing the food, Julia and Tam began picking through home-made delicacies and filling plates.

"Here, try some of this." Woody handed her a cup half-full of an amber liquid.

Julia accepted the cup and tried a sip. "Ew, what is that?"

Charlotte took the proffered cup from her hand and gave it back to Woodruff. "Woody's been trying to make beer. So far, he's the only one who likes it. But we have wine that is quite good."

"I'll try a little of that, thanks."

The music changed when another performer stepped on the stage with a violin in hand.

"Oh. oh. Wonderful!" Charlotte placed a hand on Julia's shoulder. "That's Antonio. I didn't know he was here. You'll like what's coming."

Antonio stepped to the center of the stage and drew his bow softly across the strings. A sonorous warble filled the room. Then turning to the other musicians, he nodded and began a slow, stately melody.

Wooden chairs lined two of the walls and Charlotte guided Julia and Tam to vacant ones. They all sat and watched the dancers pair up, most with smiling faces, some with nervous eyes.

Paul arrived late and found them sitting with food on their laps. "I see you've found the food."

Tam smiled over a corn cob as Julia nodded.

Paul moved a chair closer and sat with them.

They watched the dancers in comfortable silence for a while. Paul said, "I bet you didn't know Stradivarius could play, did you?"

Julia frowned and pointed at the performer with a pinky finger. "That's Stradivarius?"

Paul nodded. "He made that violin a long time ago and decided to learn to play. Good, huh?"

"Yeah, he is. Even I've heard of him," Julia said.

Paul continued, "There's a village near Damascus. A lot of musicians out of history settled there. They have a big concert about every three months. Very popular. Antonio starts his tour from there once a year."

The music changed again. As the tempo picked up, men and women paired off for a square dance. Paul stood, winked at Charlotte, and held out his hand to Julia.

Julia looked up at him with wide eyes. "What? Oh, I've not danced in a long time."

Charlotte took her half-empty plate. "This is a good time to try it again, wouldn't you say?"

Julia glanced at Tam, then out to the floor. "You might need to pick me up off the floor a few times, but okay."

"Alright, an adventurous spirit," Paul encouraged.

A man in overalls went to center stage and began calling the dance moves. The afternoon wore on as Julia danced and Tam went outside to play with other children.

Julia slept at Charlotte's place that night. Tam slept on the back porch with two hound dogs and a family of cats. A makeshift bed from a canvas bag stuffed with moss had been set out for him.

By early morning they were back on the road headed east toward Turkey and closer to Tam's family.

Caleb woke with his customary stillness, just a languid lifting of his eyelids. The sun was starting to rise, though it made little difference. The light from the tower seventy miles away gave the entire landscape a dusky ambiance. He, Chen, and Jake had slept near the beach under native palm trees. Smoke from morning fires defined the distance to the town of Alexandria a half-mile away.

They had met a fisherman yesterday who offered to take them through the marshes to the east of Egypt's delta, about a day's trip. The fisherman, Otto, sat nearby mending a net as he waited for them to rise.

"Breakfast?" he asked.

Chen sat up. "Sure, what do you have?"

"Fish, of course, and grain soup," he said.

Caleb sat up next and looked around.

Jake groaned from where he still lay on the ground. "I think I had a nightmare. That angel showed up again."

Caleb looked over at him. "Really?"

"Yeah, but it ended okay. He didn't stab me this time; he only stabbed Chen."

"You're welcome. Glad to be of service," Chen retorted.

"Anytime," Jake said as he rose and stretched.

Otto stirred glowing embers under a dented metal pot. "Food's ready." He produced four bowls, divvied up the contents of the pot, and handed the bowls around. "If you don't like it, don't say anything."

Chen sipped the broth and looked up. "This is good."

The others said likewise and finished in short order.

Caleb said to Otto, "We'd like to get going as soon as you're ready. If we hurry, we can be at the tower in a couple of days."

Otto put his net down on the sand as he considered. "The tower entrance is over a week away, even if you take a boat up the coastline."

"But the southern wall is only two days away." Jake pointed north to the tower wall rising in the distance.

Chen frowned. "Are you going to say there is no southern entrance?"

"Yes, of course. Everyone knows there is only one entrance, and it is in the north wall near Nablus."

Caleb sighed. "Why didn't I know that? We'll either need to walk around to the east or take a boat up the west coast."

"I'm up for walking. I've had enough of ships," Chen said quickly.

"Me, too," Jake said.

"Fine by me. Let's get to the east side of these marshes and head across country. I figure two days to the tower, three days around the east wall of the tower and maybe a couple to the north entrance."

Thanks to Otto's generosity they had reached the other side of the marshes by evening and disembarked. They stood on the bank and waved goodbye to their ride and looked east toward a flat open desert. To Caleb's bemusement, the desert was not the seemingly sterile parched land of a millennium ago but was heavy in scattered bushes and high thin trees. They checked their water bottles and started out northeast, the tower unmistakable, rising out of the ground in the distance like a mountain of metal and stone, almost straight up, monopolizing the horizon, reflecting and deflecting wind and clouds.

Jake said, "I could not have imagined this. It is way bigger than I thought."

"And we're still fifty miles away," Caleb said.

"Yeah." Jake shielded his eyes and looked further up, trying to find the top, but only saw more tower rising through the sky to disappear into the clouds, with no end in sight.

After a few hours of walking through low brush and high trees, they came upon an animal trail heading in the right direction. Caleb called a halt and they found soft sand under some bushes and slept soundly till the next morning. Then taking the trail, they stayed on it till noon, where they found an oasis, large and occupied by a herd of wild horses and other desert animals.

Chen stopped at the water's edge and glanced around the perimeter of the wide pool of clear water. Then he shucked off his pack and belt and waded in. Then lying prone in the water, he waved in invitation to his friends.

"Good thing there are no alligators, hunh?" Caleb said loudly.

Chen sat up in the shallow water. "Alligators?"

"No. No alligators. Enjoy yourself, Chen. I'm going to sit right here." Jake sat on the dry bank and removed his boots and socks. He dipped a boot in the water and, filling it, dumped it over his head and face. "Ah, that's how we do it where I'm from."

Caleb stood by them watching the horses and thinking. After a few minutes, he said, "I'll be right back," and walked away toward the horses.

As Caleb approached the herd, a large black stallion moved to meet him, effectively shielding the mares. Caleb stepped cautiously closer, with open hands and words of good intentions. When he was a few feet away, he stood still and waited. The stallion closed the gap and sniffed him all over, then stepped away, allowing an older mare to take his place. She sniffed once, then nickered at him as if greeting one of her own.

As Chen and Jake watched, Caleb talked with the stallion and the alpha mare for a good ten minutes, then he walked back with the stallion, ten mares, and two foals following.

"Who's your new friends?" Jake asked.

"Chen, Jake, this is... ah, his name is way too long to pronounce ... and I don't know how to translate it anyway. Let's just call him 'Chester'. That's close enough. This is his family. He offered to give us a ride. Not him, but his ladies will."

Chen perked up and stood up in the water. "Hey. Good. My feet were getting tired."

The stallion whinnied and three mares separated from the others and ambled over to stand by the men. Chen placed a hand on a speckled mare's neck. "Beautiful creature, yes?"

"Sure thing," Jake said and introduced himself to another mare.

"It's been a long time, guys," Caleb said as he smoothed his hand across his mare's back. "Let's find out how this is going to work."

Chen patted his mare's back and nimbly jumped up and straddled her back. She skittered a little and settled down. The others

did the same and the stallion turned and headed northeast, his herd following.

As they left the pool behind, Jake called out. "Hey Boss, what do we have to do in return for all this generosity?"

"When we get as far as they're going, we get to give them all a really good rubdown. Except for the stallion, he needs to keep his dignity."

Chen chuckled. "Sounds about right."

As the afternoon wore on the shadows lengthened and the horses continued steadily east, the wall of the tower only a few miles away, but appearing much closer. As they passed by, they noticed many structures built against the wall, some of them multi-story. Caleb tried to imagine how it must have been built. During his career in the army, he'd worked with engineers. This structure could easily have taken all of mankind with every last dreg of resources of every civilization ten thousand years to build, if they knew how--which they didn't, in Caleb's opinion. He knew the south wall was about fifty miles across, which meant the other three walls probably were, too. No matter how much he thought about it, he couldn't imagine what the inside must be like. He knew people lived in there--a lot of people. The famous Garden of Eden was on the ground floor. And above that? He hoped to find out. It seemed a person could spend a thousand years and not come to know a tenth of it.

Night fell and the stallion called a halt. Chen jumped off and hugged his mare, patting her neck and making soothing sounds.

Jake and Caleb both slid down carefully, staggering as they regained their footing.

"I thought my backside was tougher than that," Jake said.

"Same here," Caleb agreed with a wince.

The stallion ambled over, whinnied, and snorted at Caleb, shaking his head to flare his mane. Caleb shrugged and said, "Sure. Appreciate that."

Jake, standing by his mare with a hand on her back, asked, "What was that about?"

"Chester has offered to take us further tomorrow. His girls are tired. We rest here tonight, then head out in the morning."

Chen and Jake looked relieved at the further reprieve and eagerly set up camp. The herd grazed nearby, keeping the men company.

They rose as the sun came over the horizon and were on their way within minutes, eating travel rations in the saddle, so-to-speak.

A few hours later they rounded the edge of the tower wall, and the eastern side came into sight. The landscape had slowly changed from open desert scrub to more dense greenery. A river came into view, the remains of the old Dead Sea, now thriving with pure clean water, the banks heavy with lush trees.

They continued, the horses snatching bites from bushes as they passed. About ten miles along the tower wall, they came to the first settlement, nestled in a hollow, high among tree covered rocks by the river.

Chester whinnied and stopped, waving his head, his mane flowing.

"Looks like this is the end of our ride," Caleb said to the others. They all came to a stop and gathered by the water's edge, the horses walking out into the water and drinking, the foals playing at the water's edge.

That evening the three men spent hours rubbing down the mares and the foals with rolled up bundles of dried grass.

Caleb rubbed down one of the foals the last bit and slapped him on the butt. "There you go, little guy. How was that?" The foal scampered away whinnying and tossing his head. Caleb watched him with amazement. He could, somehow, feel the foal's light-hearted exuberance.

"I think we'll wear the hide right off them if we keep this up," Jake said, tossing his bundle of straw to the ground.

"Well. What do you think?" Caleb asked the stallion standing close by.

The stallion stared at Caleb directly in the eyes, then turned and walked away.

"I think that means we're done." Chen patted his mare one last time, went to his pack, and shrugged into the straps.

"So right," Jake said and did the same.

Waving to the stallion and his girls, they all started walking north toward the small settlement among the rocks.

Time had healed a lot of wounds in the land. Nearly a thousand years of peace, beginning with a nuclear war and ending with a spiritual war, had buried much rubble of the past and erased all organisms created by Satan's minions in their underground labs. No diseases existed that harmed people. All people now had a vastly improved body. Some could even be compared to the so-called superheroes of mythology. After weeks of walking, Caleb was not the least bit tired, he rather enjoyed the time outdoors and the new discoveries.

They came upon a trail leading upward among the building sized rocks and decided to take it to higher ground. Halfway up the trail a small shack made of local wood, rough and plain, sat twenty feet to the side of the path. An old man, the only really old man Caleb had seen since his arrival, sat cross legged at the entrance on a straw mat. His long gray beard reached to his lap and trailed to the ground.

Hoping to get better directions, Caleb stopped. "Greetings, friend," he called out.

"Greetings, Warrior Caleb Carson, Called of God." The old man smiled a crooked smile and waved to the ground where he sat. "Join me, you and your friends. We have things to discuss."

Caleb turned to his companions and raised an eyebrow. They shrugged back.

They walked over to the shack, dropped their packs to the ground, and sat by the old man on mats laid out near him.

"Beer?" the old man asked as he reached into the doorway behind him and produced a glass bottle filled with amber liquid.

Jake smiled. "Sure. Propitious timing, I'd say."

After taking a few good swallows, Caleb said slowly, "You obviously knew we were coming. I'm ready to hear what you need to say."

Jake and Chen sat quietly knowing this would relate to Caleb's mission.

The old man said, "You learned your lesson at the beach. That's good. Some don't learn so easily."

Caleb scratched the short stubble on his chin. "Yeah, that got my attention."

"I imagine you've asked yourself why God has called a man such as yourself."

Caleb nodded.

"It's not your martial experience so much as what other experiences on the battlefield have taught you."

Caleb listened carefully.

"The Lord took notice of you during your time with the army and later as a mercenary. He noticed you cared for your men. He also noticed you cared even for your enemies, the ones you didn't shoot, that is." The old man grinned.

Caleb grimaced. "Yeah, about that..."

The old man held up a hand. "Not my point, actually. I'm to tell you that you indeed have a mission, a very difficult mission. You and your companions."

Jake glanced over to Chen, who nodded back.

"Jake is right that you are not angels and there are no bad guys in this place."

Caleb frowned. What was that supposed to mean? Are there other places? Is there a part of heaven needing further cleansing? Is someone up to no good like when the devil went rogue who-knows-how-long-ago and started a rebellion? That actually made a little sense to him.

The old man continued. "One thing you learned as a man of duty and as an officer is that you rarely have all the information you believe you need; there is always a bit of faith attached to taking orders."

That Caleb knew well. He knew what it meant to crouch in a hole in the ground waiting for an airdrop or reinforcements. He knew when the general said the strategy was sound, he could either argue or assume the general knew what he was talking about.

"Are we getting into the need-to-know area?" Caleb asked.

"You can say that, except you will eventually find out all about your mission--even the why."

Jake held up a hand for attention. "You sound like you're speaking from experience."

The old man lowered his head for a moment in silence. He raised his chin and looked Caleb in the eyes. "I am Colonel Kunetzov."

Caleb's hand twitched at the name and his hand, unknowing to Caleb, curled into a fist. He rose to a knee. "You can't be Kunetzov. Kunetzov," he spit the words out, "is, is ...it's impossible. He can't be here."

Chen watching and listening carefully seemed to know where this was going. He touched Caleb on the arm. "Captain, tell Jake and me of this Kunetzov."

Caleb turned an angry glare on Chen. Then taking a deep breath, settled back on the mat. "This is personal, Chen."

Chen glared back. "I understand that. It must be something very close to your heart. But have we not traveled together? Fought together? Tell me we're not your men."

Caleb breathed deeply, not looking at the enemy sitting across from him, an enemy whose life he had sworn to end. He breathed deeply. "Yes, we fought together--and won, sort of." He let out a shallow laugh and turned his eyes on the old man. "Tell me how you can possibly be here."

Kunetzov had been staring at the ground. He answered. "I have been waiting a long time for this moment. I had much to answer for and have already done so." He looked back up to the three men. "I did not give the order. I hesitated and my lieutenant, knowing my superior's wishes, called in the strike."

"They had surrendered. They were coming out. They were my friends." Tears wet Caleb's eyes.

"I know."

"Who gave the order, then?" Caleb demanded.

"Doesn't matter. He's not in this place."

"Serves him right, the bastard," Caleb said.

"Yes, he is not here, and justice has been served, but the villagers and the resistance fighters—many are here. I found most of them and made amends long ago."

Jake asked, "Why did you hesitate? Seems clear to me. They surrendered."

"My hesitation was not about the order. My hesitation was surprise that my superior would give the order. I thought I knew him. He was my mentor."

"He chose the dark side," Chen said sadly.

"Is this why you've been sitting here waiting for us?" Caleb said.

"Possibly. I'm not sure. When I first came to this village, I sensed I would find peace here. When I first arrived, my beard was only a few inches. It has been a pleasant wait, though. The village children visit me often."

"This was planned, then. Another lesson. Was it about forgiveness? Is that what I'm supposed to learn here?" Caleb asked sourly.

"Perhaps, among other things."

The old man stood. He was short and wiry, and his beard hung below his waist. "I believe I am free to wander again. I'd like to go with you."

Sitting on the mat, Caleb watched him rise and stretch. After the old man's words hit Caleb's ears, Caleb put his hand to his forehead and laughing, realized a weight had been lifted from his spirit.

"How many lessons will there be, Kunetzov, hunh?" Caleb said, standing and picking up his pack. Jake and Chen rose, also.

Kunetzov shrugged. "I have no idea, but for me, there has been plenty. Come on, I'll introduce you to my village friends."

They continued up the path to the village among the rocks.

CHAPTER THIRTEEN

They had been traveling for four days since the morning breakfast at the small Greek village of Dilovaci.

Anna, Oscar, Helen, and Sandon had stopped by a river's edge to replenish their water bags. When they left Greece the day before, they took a boat to the opposite shore into Turkey and were now already well inland near the abandoned city of Pergamos. They could see the ruins in the distance.

"You know the story of this city, right?" Sandon asked the others. He sat on soft grass at the water's edge and put his feet in to cool them.

"All I know is Satan had his headquarters here for a while," Oscar said.

"Our Lord has preserved a portion of the ruins for now. Best we see them and remember the lessons learned."

Sandon lay back on the grass. "I remember the day I heard of Satan's transgression. I was with friends relaxing with food and drink. I had a hard time believing it. I looked up to Lucifer then; he was the signet of perfection, full of wisdom and beauty. He had access to the throne and was often in Our Lord's presence.

"I still don't understand much of what happened. One day we received word that Lucifer had abandoned his post and fled to a remote location. I'd never heard of the place, but Our Lord knew where, of course. So, my commander approached me and said we were preparing for war. The great armory was opened, and awful weapons rolled forth.

"Michael, our general, gave a speech about light and dark. He explained a little about Satan's desire to split off and start his own society. Satan was in a hurry. He didn't have time to gain followers by asking for volunteers, he was content with slaves.

"Great energies flew across heaven. Edifices toppled and war machines evaporated in flashes the size of worlds. The war quickly went sour for him even though he had many of my fellows tricked into following him. Most abandoned him when they realized what he truly wanted. He eventually fled here hoping to raise a more powerful army. The rest is in the scriptures.

"I still feel sad at the thought, even though all things have now been made right and there is peace."

"When did this happen?" Oscar asked.

"Oh, Lucifer had been causing problems for a long time. He understood at least a part of God's overall plan. After the garden was put here, Adam and Eve were put in charge of keeping it and replenishing the world. Lucifer thought he had ruined God's plan then, but later, after our Lord rose from the dead, Lucifer saw he had severely misunderstood God's strategy and had lost. All that was left to him was war."

"Oh," Helen said, sadly shaking her head.

"Why did God let Satan walk right in and screw things over?" Anna asked. "Seems He could have ended it then."

"My brothers and I have speculated much about that. So, we asked. The answer was very satisfying and shows us more about the true nature of our God. Adam was to be the beginning of a new race. Adam and Eve, though modeled after us heavenly beings, were made to live here and be keepers of this world. They were given near total control of their destiny and freedom to grow and make end-less choices for right and wrong. Real people, with real truth flowing through their veins, based on real choices they made. They were the kernel of a new race, but they would only mature if allowed to choose between good and evil, God or Lucifer. So, he was allowed to stay on Earth."

Anna threw a stick in the water and watched it float away. "You said the other day something about striving to relinquish beliefs that are not completely true. If we were able to do that, what would be the end result? What would we be? Would we even be human?"

"Of course, you would," Sandon laughed. "Human is more than what you've experienced so far. Humans are capable of so much more. It starts with the mind. You must take out the false and put in the true, then you will have 'the mind of Christ', as scripture says."

Helen had been leaning against a tree. She pushed away and picked up her pack and water bag. "I say let's get away from this creepy place. I'm getting nauseous."

"Me too." Oscar rose from the grass.

Anna, lying on the grass, leaned up on an elbow. "What about you, Sandon? Are you ready to get going? We can head straight for Antioch and be there in three days or we can take a ship to Cypress and cut a few more days off the trip."

"Whatever you guys want. I'm just here in case you need something I can supply." Sandon rose and offered a hand to Anna. She took it and he pulled her to her feet. "So, south to the coast or east to Syria?"

Anna hefted her pack. "Let's go east. I'm curious. And I don't care for the water much."

They headed east, skirting the dead ruins of Satan's former glory, and found a dirt road heading east and a little south.

Western Turkey was a surprise to Julia. She had always thought of it as rocks and dry tundra, but to her relief, it was pleasant and cool most of the time, if not a little cold in the early morning. She and Tam sat by a fire they had built by rocky ruins on a hill over-looking the city of Antioch. They had made great progress the past few days due to the wagon and driver who gave them a ride.

"Three more days of walking and we'll be in Tarsus," Julia said.

Tam looked up from the stick he held in the fire with a short section of corncob roasting on it.

"You don't look thrilled. Worried about something?"

Tam nodded.

"Want to tell me about it?"

Tam looked up, a frown creasing his usually unworried eyes. "They might all be grown up."

"Who might be grown?" Julia asked.

"Alexander and Rufus, my brothers." Tam turned his stare back to the fire.

"Why would you think that?"

Tam stayed silent for a minute. "The men on the wagon said sometimes kids grow up in Paradise before they come here. I didn't. But they might be all grown and big. I'm still just a kid. What if they don't want to be around me?"

"Tam, that's not going to happen. This is heaven. The Lord knows all about us. I'll bet your brothers are just like they were when you were little."

"What if they grew up and had kids? What if they're old men?" Tears wet Tam's face.

Julia scooted closer to him. "I hadn't considered that, Tam. Still, they would be more than glad to see you. You would remind them of all the fun they had when they were your age. They will love to be with you. That's for sure."

"You think so?"

"Yeah, I do. So, let's pack our gear and head east. Tarsus is only a few days away. Hey, maybe we'll get a ride again, hunh?"

A few minutes later they were on the road headed down the hill to the village of Antioch. As they approached, they saw a tractor in a far field pulling a hay wagon. Steam billowed up from a tall stack and big iron wheels turned slowly. They came to the edge of the village. White plastered homes contrasted with stone huts and more modern brick and mortar homes, all on the same street. Tam pointed to streetlights installed on the corners of homes or at the street corners, his wide eyes taking it all in.

Julia said, "Looks like someone here understands this modern stuff. Electric lights--I kind of like them. A lot brighter than sodium lamps."

People waved or nodded as they walked by. They passed a confectionary shop. Its door was propped open with an old clothing iron.

Julia gripped Tam's arm. "Hey, kiddo, want to try something tasty for a change?"

Tam stopped and stared through the window at donuts arranged on a shelf. "They have holes in them."

"Yeah, true, but they still taste good. Come on, let's try one."

They stepped through the door to the delicious smell of lemon, chocolate, and vanilla. A young woman smiled as they went to the counter. "What kind of money do you take?" Julia asked.

"Oh, almost anything. What do you have?" she responded.

"I have a few silvers left and a few gold coins." Julia pulled her purse around and stirred the contents with her fingers.

"May I see a silver?" she asked, holding out her hand.

"Sure." Julia handed over a silver coin.

Examining it, the proprietor said, "This coin is large. I'd say five donuts or three chocolate flimsies."

Julia asked, "What's a flimsy? I've never heard of that."

"Oh, you'll love them. I invented them myself. Hold on. I'll be right back." She disappeared into a back room and came back with a plate of flat round cookies.

"Here, try one. The first is free."

Julia reached for a cookie and tried to pick it up, but it sagged in her fingers. "Yeah, I see why you call them that." Taking a bite, she smiled, then tore a piece off and handed it to Tam.

Taking a bite, Tam's face lit up. "I like that. Let's buy some."

"Don't you want a donut?" Julia asked.

"No, let's get these. They're really good."

Julia shrugged. "We'll get some of both." She handed over another silver. "Five donuts and three flimsies."

Walking out of the shop, Tam and Julia noticed little of the village as they ate the sweets. They came to the edge of town and stopped to get drinks and fruit from a vendor at a vegetable stand. Then they continued east. Along the way, they occasionally met other travelers. Wagons pulled by mules and oxen passed them traveling both ways with waves from total strangers, laden with produce, hay, or lumber tightly bound. The road seemed to be getting better.

The day passed. The next day found them on a paved road, irregular stones interspersed with loose rocks. They saw more electric lights, too. The day after, the stone road met with the black of asphalt and the sound of rubber wheels on pavement and small electric trucks and cars zipped by with a low frequency hum. A half-hour after taking the paved road, heading more south than east, a car with an open top stopped and offered a ride.

"Where you going?" A young Turkish man smiled from behind a steering wheel shaped like a large rubber horseshoe.

"We're going to Tarsus," Julia said. "Is this the right way?"

"Tarsus, huh?" the young man said. "Yes, Tarsus is this way. It's on the old Highway 51. You are now on Highway 21. I'm going east. I can take you part of the way."

"Thank you, sir." They got in the car and introduced themselves. The car hum rose in pitch, and they continued down the road at a speed much faster than each felt comfortable with.

"You like my car?" the young man asked with a smile and lift of his chin.

"It's very fast." Julia held her hair down with a hand on her shoulder.

"Yes, I made this car myself. Worked on it for eight years. It'll go faster, but I see you're not comfortable. I'll slow down for you." He grinned and slowed down minutely. "Is that better?"

"Ah, yes. Thank you," Julia said with her hand still on her shoulder.

Tam, sitting in the back seat, leaned forward. "What makes it go so fast?"

"That, my friend," the driver glanced back, "is called an engine, or motor—take your pick. This one is electric, driven by a field coil tuned to the ether at seven point eight six cycles. It self-charges if I keep my speed low enough, but I rarely do," he chuckled.

"I don't understand." Tam leaned closer.

"Most of my friends don't either, but down south near Damascus they have lots of these guys. It's a new thing. Someone is starting a factory. That's where I'm going. I'm going to show them my concept of ether entrapment. It's way different from the usual way of tuning."

"I didn't understand that either." Tam frowned.

"Don't worry, you'll get it later."

He drove in silence for a moment as Tam and Julia watched the trees and brush pass swiftly by.

"So, what's your story?" The driver broke the silence.

"I'm going to find my family," Tam said.

"Oh yeah? They're in Tarsus?"

"We think so," Julia said.

"I know people in Tarsus. I have family there. So, who are you looking for? Maybe I can help point the way."

"Simon of Cyrene is my dad. We're looking for him first, I guess," Tam said.

The driver turned in his seat, glancing back at the road. "Grandpa Simon is your dad?"

Tam let go of the front seat back and leaned back in his seat. "Ah."

"Did you say Simon of Cyrene? He's my great, great grandfather. HA! That would make you my granduncle Tam. I thought the name sounded familiar. Granddad Simon brings up the name every once in a while. Whoa, I gotta slow down. I'm taking you all the way to Tarsus. Wait till they see you. Granddad's been waiting for you to get here for a long time. This is gonna be great. I gotta see this."

Frowning in confusion, Tam asked, "So, who are you?"

"I'm Anzul. Evidently, you're my uncle. Weird, hunh?"

"This is happening way too fast," Julia said. "Let's get to Tarsus and ask them, just to make sure."

"Yeah, okay. Sorry, I get carried away sometimes." Ten minutes later they turned west on Highway 51 and within five minutes pulled into a long stone driveway leading into a copse of large trees with five buildings nestled in the shade.

They came to an abrupt stop and the silence was a welcome relief. Julia got out and stood on the solid ground taking comfort from the lack of motion. Tam climbed out after her. Anzul walked around the car and said, "Come on. Let me introduce you and see what's what."

The house they approached was built of cut stone, white, streaked with a scatter of blue and green blotches. Shadows from the high trees created shades of greens and grays.

Approaching the front open door, Anzul called out. "Grandfather, grandmother." Hearing nothing, he turned and walked around the house toward the back where a patio and swimming pool had been cut from bedrock. Tam and Julia followed closely behind, Tam gripping Julia's hand tightly.

As they approached, they saw two young men sitting by the pool, one with feet in the water, the other with a book in his hands reading aloud to the other. They turned. Seeing Anzul, they paused, then seeing Tam and Julia they rose to their feet and smiling, rushed forward to embrace Tam, shouting welcomes.

"Tam, we've been waiting for you. We just got here a week ago. Father knew you must be coming soon. Come on. Father's at the olive press." Rufus, now with an apparent age of seventeen, put an arm around his younger brother and they walked around the pool and up a path toward a low roofed shed cut in the hillside.

Alexander, fifteen, said in amazement, "Tam, you look exactly the same as when we were in Jerusalem."

"I do? You're bigger," Tam said, looking up at his older brother.

"I know. Alexander and I were killed in the fighting a few years later. But Rufus got married and had a girl. She survived. That's how Anzul is here."

When they reached the low building, Rufus called," Father. Come outside, please."

A few seconds later Simon stepped from the dusky interior and stood in the doorway. "What...?" Seeing young Tam standing by his older brother, Simon heaved a sigh of relief and, smiling, held out his arms.

Tam ran to him, nearly knocking him over. Tears wet his eyes and Julia's too. Soon they all were crying for joy and smiling.

"Your mother will be home in a few days. She will be overjoyed," Simon said. Turning his attention on Julia, he said, "Who is your friend, Tam?"

"This is Julia. She's been helping me."

Simon hugged her. "Thank you, Julia, for bringing Tam back to us," he said fervently.

Julia smiled, but with a wisp of sadness. Her journey with Tam was over. She was at loose ends now, not sure what the next step would be.

Simon was still speaking, "...and you can stay with us if you like. We have plenty of space here. This is a great community to live in. A lot of first century citizens are here. We're comfortable with sticking to the old ways."

Julia nodded her head, unwilling to speak just yet.

Simon clapped his hands. "Alright, time for a celebration. Tam is home!" He put a hand on Alexander's shoulder. "Go tell the neighbors. We're having a homecoming party."

Alexander smiled and with a light punch on Tam's shoulder, as if they were both kids again, rushed away to tell the good news.

CHAPTER FOURTEEN

Caleb, Chen, and Jake spent a day in Kunetzov's village gathering supplies and saying farewells. Many of the residents of the hamlet were surprised to see Kunetzov out and about. He rarely left the shack he lived in.

They bartered with a local for a few days of rations.

Caleb fidgeted as he waited; he liked to keep things rolling and hated to have unanswered questions hanging over his head. "So, you ready to hit the trail?"

Kunetzov tightened the strap on his makeshift pack, his gray beard hanging down past his belt, and stepped outside the village store. He looked around one last time. "Yeah, I suppose so. I've been here a long time. It grows on you, you know."

Jake and Chen, who were standing outside watching the natives, so-to-speak, roused when they appeared.

Caleb told them, "The leader here says a large town has grown up around the entrance to the tower. It'll take a day to round the northeast corner, then about a day's walk to get to it."

An hour later they were well away from the hamlet and heading north, always keeping the tower wall within throwing distance. A well-worn trail, more like a dirt road, led them meandering around outcrops of rock and around hills, but in the right general direction.

By nightfall, the trail led them close to the tower wall and around the corner. They saw a glow in the sky from the town twenty miles away.

A sign had been erected on the road with a large red arrow pointing west. It read, "Eden City, Welcome All."

"Eden City, hunh?" Jake asked curiously, looking around at the others.

Kunetzov muttered something about not remembering the sign.

They stopped there, pulled out their packs, and settled down for the night, waking as the sun came up. After a brief breakfast, they shrugged their packs on and started west.

Eighteen miles later they came to the first signs of city life. It was past noon and warm. The tower, only two hundred yards away, rose up, encompassing the entire southern sky. A street vendor selling cool drinks and snacks had a large sign by the stone paved road. The sign read, "Street of the Apostles".

They stopped for drinks and rested, then continued. The further they walked, the more they saw that the last description of the town they got was out of date by at least thirty years. Continuous construction had been going on for a long time and the locals said the gate was still five miles further west on this street they'd entered on. The buildings were getting larger and more permanent, made from stone, which was plentiful in the area, or brick and concrete. Also, those who built had permanency in mind. The closer to the center of what Caleb now considered a small city, as the sign had said, the more highly embellished the buildings were with murals and symbols incorporated into their design. Further on, multistory buildings came into view, then buildings ten stories high.

After a few more miles the buildings of the city rose up twenty and thirty floors. Those hugging the tower were even higher and reminded Caleb of vines clinging to a tree and growing upward for light. The Street of the Apostles widened to four lanes and Caleb realized they were approaching the main thoroughfare.

They stopped at the intersection on the main avenue and stared in wonder. To the left the main avenue ended in two blocks, the tower entrance standing open and inviting. To the right, heading north, the main avenue continued as far as they could see. Monumental pillars were set to each side of the avenue hundreds of feet high and twenty feet wide at the base. Across the street, he saw the entrance to the university with many imposing structures of stone and wood. Everywhere were signs of religious interest. Roofs of buildings held scripture quotations running along the cornices in bas relief. Crosses were everywhere. The names of the apostles were the street signs. Against the tower wall, the tallest building rose a three hundred feet, mimicking the stony metallic texture and color of the tower itself.

The streets were full of citizens moving about, most walking with a casual saunter. Every era and civilization seemed to be represented with clashing colors and styles. It almost gave Caleb a headache.

"Okay, so here we are," Caleb said." Where to now?"

"Let's stop somewhere and get something hot to eat and cold to drink," Jake suggested.

From the corner they stood on, they saw no less than eight eating establishments.

"Considering how dirty we are, I'd suggest we stay out of high-class places," Chen said.

"I know of a place, if they're still open," Kunetzov said, "Follow me." He led them a block past the gray stone structures of the university complex, and two blocks away from the university.

Kunetzov pointed. "I used to love this place. A Russian owned it, of course. He made very good stroganoff." They stopped at a three-story brick building used as a hotel. The bottom floor was the cafe Kunetzov remembered.

They walked through the front door to a crowded room filled with tables and students. Near the back wall, tables had been pulled together and a professor sat near the wall and taught, holding his students enraptured.

"Not the way I remember," Kunetzov said, a little disappointed.

"Let's check out the food anyway," Jake said.

No tables were available, most being used by students with books laid open and taking notes. The bar had space, though, so they made their way to it and sat on the stools.

A man behind the counter dressed in an apron and white shirt finished wiping the counter and stepped over. "What'll you have, friends?"

"Something to drink and whatever you have that's fast," Caleb said.

He pulled out a pad. "We have ice water, coffee, tea, beer, sodas."

"Ice water sounds good, then a beer," Chen said.

Jake lifted a hand. "Same here."

Caleb watched his three friends, then said," Water and beer for four and a menu."

The owner came back and passed drinks around." Are you men new to Eden City?"

Caleb nodded. "Just got here an hour ago."

"I see," he said, placing a couple of menus down.

"This used to be a Russian cafe," Kunetzov said. "Where's old Dimitri?"

"You *are* new around here. Dimitri took the walk about twenty years ago, but not before giving me the recipe for his stroganoff."

Jake asked, "The walk? What walk is that?"

The owner paused a moment. "He made the big leap. He walked into the tower. He entered the tower."

"Why am I not getting good vibes right now?" Caleb muttered softly to Kunetzov.

Chen, polite, as always, interjected, "Sir, I was under the impression that getting into the Garden of Eden was the eventual goal of every man. Is it so difficult as that?"

"Ah, well, it's not difficult to actually do it. It's just...it's hard to explain. Ah, hold on, look at the menus. I'll be right back."

A few minutes later he came back. "Alright, what'll you have?"

They gave their orders. Chen asked, "Have you considered my question?"

"Sure. I asked Professor Kendrick to help explain it. He's over there with his students."

Chen frowning, nodded. "Thank you."

The owner paused and leaned forward. "You men seem to be a little more than casual visitors. Are you planning on trying the walk?"

Closing the menu, Jake said, "We got no choice. He hooked a thumb toward Caleb. "He's got to go in. It was an order."

The owner's eyes went wide, and he turned and walked away. A few minutes later he returned with the professor. Both were excited.

"This is Professor Kendrick. He's..."

"Hello, gentlemen," the professor interrupted. "I'm Professor Kendrick, dean of Edenic Studies at the university. Which one of you is 'the called'?"

Caleb gave Jake a withering glance.

Jake held up both hands. "Sorry, boss."

Caleb leaned back on his stool. "That would be me."

"Oh, we're so glad to have you here. We would consider it an honor if you would stay at the university, you and your friends. We meet very few of 'the called.'"

Kunetzov interrupted. "That's all fine and good, but could I order some Stroganoff? It's been a long, long time."

The professor went back to his table after profuse apologies and a promise to meet them later at the university. Their food was delivered on steaming plates rather quickly.

"This stroganoff is amazing,"Jake said around a mouthful."

Chen lifted his fork to his mouth, then stopped to study the noodles."Are these Asian? They look like Asian noodles."

Kunetzov pointed his fork at Chen."No, they aren't Asian. The orient isn't the only place that knew how to make decent noodles. These are Russian, through and through. Now take a bite and prove me right."

Chen chewed for a few seconds. "Reminds me of my grandmother's cooking. The Russians probably got the recipe from the Japanese."

Kunetzov groaned. "Chen, don't take away an old man's last fantasy. That's not a nice thing."

Caleb paused with his fork over his plate. "Talk about fantasy. I'm not sure what the professor thinks he'll learn from me. I'm no expert on what the king of the planet has planned. But I think we should take him up on his offer. A shower and a comfy bed do sound good for a change. And I'm thinking we need to get a little advice before waltzing right into the tower. I'm getting strange vibes around here."

CHAPTER FIFTEEN

It had been weeks since Elder left Captain Newton at the docks in Greece. He sat at a table at a street-side stand munching on fried potatoes, unimpressed by the flavor and the texture, but he was hungry and tasteless potatoes filled the void in his belly. He'd taken a table by the outside wall of a storefront and leaned back against the old brick, watching people pass by and occasionally wondering where they were going and what they were doing this early in the morning.

He'd lost forty pounds in the intervening weeks, and he felt the difference. At first, he'd taken public transport when he could, but he missed so much interesting stuff, passing by too fast. So, after a few days, he started walking, instead, remembering that his reason for being in New Jerusalem was to discover what was not evident from high up on the side of Mount Olympus.

He often thought of the dry canvas he'd almost finished and not touched in a year. He remembered how he felt when Chen told him why the painting was not ready. It was like a punch to the gut. Elder realized now he'd been afraid of coming here.

He turned in his chair and looked south. The tower rose magnificent, straight as an arrow up through the clouds. Even on a rainy day such as this, it was unmistakable.

A thought occurred to him, and he frowned. Then bringing his eyes back to the people, he began to notice something he missed. He'd always felt more comfortable with the big picture. He was very good at seeing the big picture and getting it down on canvas, but learning to see the detail, at least in the way people act, was new to him. He glanced at the tower, then turned his head and followed the street to where it passed him and continued north. Of course, the street ran south to north.

No, in the context of his new idea, it ran from north to south.

He sat for another hour watching and he saw something new. Many people passed by heading in every direction, but when someone stopped, almost never did they present their back to the tower. Almost everyone unconsciously oriented themselves so they could at least see the tower through their peripheral vision. Interesting. What caused that? Is everyone so conscious of the tower their subconscious directs how they sit or how they stand? Or is there a power coming from the tower telling them to act this way?

Elder stood and paid for another bag of potatoes, ignoring the flavor as he walked up the street, thinking through this puzzle.

It never became totally dark within the walls of this city. Elder knew this. Even on an overcast day such as this, there was always enough light to see where you were going.

Elder sighed and munched. He thought, "Always enough light to…" he paused and stood for a full minute half in the street, his snack forgotten. His brows rose, his eyes wide. He muttered, "It's got to be the light. The light isn't right."

A few minutes later, he was on the road going west with his backpack slung over his shoulder headed for Mount Olympus and the perch high up the mountain where, many years ago, he'd seen the city as it is and his vision of what it will be.

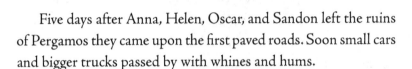

Five days after Anna, Helen, Oscar, and Sandon left the ruins of Pergamos they came upon the first paved roads. Soon small cars and bigger trucks passed by with whines and hums.

"What do you think of those vehicles?" Sandon asked the group.

"I was raised in Germany in 1984," Oscar said. They were starting to experiment with electricity for cars. Nice. Better than petrol motors."

"Better than horse pulled carriages, too—maybe," Helen said.

Anna watched another car rush by stirring her hair. "Might as well be magic as far as I can tell. There was nothing like this in Rome at my time. Chariots or a good horse was the fastest way of traveling."

Sandon watched a car disappear in the distance. "Yet, there are faster ways of traveling than this. There is a lesson here. Think on this."

"What now, Sandon? Which way?" Anna asked.

Antioch is a day's walk, but I think we should get you used to a faster mode of travel."

Sandon stepped out into the road and held out a hand.

"Anna started to step out with him but stepped back quickly to the edge of the road. "Sandon, you're going to get run over."

"All will be well, Anna," Sandon said from the middle of the road.

A few seconds later a small twenty-seat bus came to a stop and the door opened.

Sandon peered inside to see three other passengers. "Mind if we ride with you?" Sandon asked the driver.

"Come on in." The driver waved them in cheerfully.

Sandon selected seats for them in the middle of the bus and they settled in.

Anna sat gripping the seat back in front of her.

"Sit back and enjoy, Anna, Helen. We'll be in Antioch in an hour." Sandon leaned back and stretched his long legs out into the aisle.

After a few minutes of watching scenery rushing by, Helen asked, "This is very fast. Are we in a hurry?"

"Not really," Sandon said. "When we enter the tower, you will find many amazing things. This will help you adjust. This is only the beginning."

"Will we be going faster than this?" Anna asked.

"Yes, if you are ready for it."

"Wow." Anna didn't know what else to say.

An hour later they entered Antioch, then continued through town and into open country.

"I thought we were going to Antioch," Oscar said.

Sandon smiled. "Are you hungry already? We've only been traveling an hour."

"Well, where does this vehicle go to?" Helen asked.

"All the way to the tower--it or another vehicle like it. I'm thinking we keep going 'til we get into Galilee. That would be about another five hours."

After a while, Anna said, "This is so fast," and fell asleep.

The meal did wonders and Kunetzov's delight at the stroganoff was not misplaced. Caleb felt energized again and amazed he felt no stiff muscles or strained tendons. Standing outside the cafe, they watched pedestrians walk past. A few electric vehicles were parked near the curb. A truck, passing them slowly, pulled to a stop fifty feet away. Two men got out, went to the back, and unloaded produce onto the sidewalk near the cafe door.

"Electric cars and electric streetlights." Jake pointed to a street-light mounted on the side of the building. "I wonder if the whole city is run by battery or if they have a generator somewhere? The ether has got to be really strong, right here by the tower."

Kunetzov shrugged. "Last time I was here, fifty years ago, there were none I knew about. That's progress, I suppose."

"I say we look around a bit." Jake pointed down the street.

"You guys go ahead. I want to check out the university," Caleb said.

After a few minutes of deciding where to rendezvous, Caleb and Chen headed toward the university. Jake and Kunetzov went the other direction.

As they approached the campus, Caleb saw that the university consisted of only two buildings, both very large and imposing structures of stone with clay tile roofs three stories high. They went to the first building, its entrance being on a side street. Walking in, they were met by a young man dressed in a robe of a single cloth. A cross hung on a chain around his neck.

"Hello friends," the monk said.

Caleb paused at the sight of the monk. "Were looking for Professor Kendrick."

The monk pulled out a brass watch on a chain. "He should be returning from lunch any time now. His office is in the main building. This building is the living quarters. Are you passing through?"

"Yeah, we're visiting Eden City. We met the professor at the cafe. He invited us to meet with him."

The monk raised a brow. "Oh really? I'll ask." He went to a desk and pulled a small speaker from a box mounted on the wall, put it to his mouth, and turned a crank a few revolutions. "Clarence, is Professor Kendrick back from lunch? Okay." He placed the speaker on the hook and came back. "The professor is in his office in the main building. Just go in the front entrance. Someone will direct you."

As they walked across the clipped grass, Caleb commented," That seemed really strange. Why have a monastery in heaven? Why not just go through the entrance? Surely answers are better found in there."

"Monks are often very guarded men. I've known a few. A Buddhist monastery was near my home in my youth," Chen said.

"Well, something about that guy bothered me."

They came to the front entrance of the main building facing out on the wide boulevard. Caleb stopped and studied the sights around him. Two blocks away the entrance to the tower stood stark and dark like a tunnel into a mountain. At least fifty feet high and thirty wide, the entrance held no doors. It was always open, evidently. High pillars twenty feet wide at the base bracketed the entrance and rose up high, capped by statues of animals in peaceful repose. Caleb started counting the columns as he turned his head and finally stopped at sixty-eight as they faded out of sight up the boulevard to the north where the main entrance to the city was.

One block from the dark tower entrance, the first side street held a bustling crowd of shoppers buying trinkets to remember their visit to Eden City. As he watched, a man dressed in rags approached the entrance and stood staring up into the dark tunnel, then slowly walked toward it, picking up speed till he was running as he disappeared inside. Many people in the crowd paused in their shopping to watch. Some continued to shop, but a few put down the wares and walked away from the crowd, head low, almost weeping.

"Well, that was strange," Chen said.

"Yeah, that guy was having a hard time of it. Better to run through the entrance than lose courage halfway there."

Chen glanced up at Caleb. "I have seen strong men cry when faced with their own lack of courage."

"I've seen enough. Let's go visit the professor." Caleb turned around and headed up stone steps, Chen following.

They entered into dim light. A ceiling fan spun lazily overhead. A central hallway bisected the main building letting a cool breeze waft through from the central courtyard, which could be seen as a smear of green through wide doors at the far end.

A desk sat to the side and the monk there rose and bowed. "You must be 'the called'. Follow me." He turned and headed down the wide hallway. Halfway there, he stepped onto a staircase. They climbed to the third and highest floor and found the professor's office at the front of the building overlooking the main boulevard, with a clear view of the tower entrance and the street.

When they entered the office, the professor was just turning away from the window.

"Please be seated, gentlemen. Clarence, would you please bring drinks?"

The monk bowed and left Caleb and Chen standing in the middle of the large office. Caleb looked around the office, at the booklined walls and artifacts of religious significance—a cross hanging on the wall, a section of wood in a small glass case, a piece of bone from a dead saint from long ago.

The professor stood with palms together and smiled. "Ah, you see my collection. This is only a small part, however. Please be seated. We have much to discuss."

"Thank you, Professor," Caleb said.

He waved a hand at the seats. "No need for the 'professor' tag. 'Dr. Kendrick' will do."

They sat in comfortable chairs arranged in front of an ornate mahogany desk.

"Do you expect to be long in the city?" The professor leaned back in the ornate chair across the desk from them.

"Only long enough to gather information and get a few answers," Caleb said, settling into his chair.

"Ah, yes. We all want answers." The professor propped his elbows on the desk and steepled his fingers.

After an awkward silence, Caleb asked, "What did you want to discuss?"

"Everything." The professor leaned forward eagerly. "How you were called. The circumstances behind it. Why you were called and not someone else. How you know it was a true calling. I want to understand the mechanism, the formula, if you will, of the nature of Callings in general. I'm fascinated by the idea of God calling someone, a mere human to a special task."

Caleb sat in confused silence for a minute. "I'm not sure I can help you. I don't know why I was called. An angel showed up at the village I was reborn in and told me to come here. I'm nothing special."

"Oh, that's what almost everyone says. You must have a special ability or unusual knowledge. There must be something about you that sets you apart."

Caleb shrugged. "I'm telling you. I don't have a clue. I've been thinking about this for three months. I'll be just as surprised as anyone else."

"I think I know." Chen had leaned back in his chair and listened quietly. He also had thought long and hard about this whole thing.

"Oh?" the professor said, a brow raised.

Caleb turned to him, a question in his eyes.

"Alright. I know this may sound simple, but here it is. Caleb is one of the few who have volunteered. He cares. That's it. The Lord uses people who want to be used. That's why he was called. Sure, he has life experience that sets him apart from most people, but he is available for the hard work, the hardship if necessary. He gets up in the morning with a goal--to make a reasonable difference—a meaningful difference."

"You're right, that answer does sound a tad too easy," Dr. Kendrick said dismissively. "I believe life is so much more complex."

"Maybe you're complicating it too much," Caleb suggested.

The professor rose and walked to the window. "I've looked out of this window for the last eighty years, studying this subject, among others. When I was reborn right after the last war, I woke in a town in Chile. It took me sixty years to get to here. At the time this was a village of a hundred shacks, no electricity and no plumbing. I watched this village grow into a small town, then into this small city. I've seen thousands walk through the gate into the tower. And many more thousands turn away at the last minute. I've always wondered why. My life's goal is to know why."

"Have you ever stood down there at the gate, yourself?" Chen asked.

The professor whirled around. "Of course, I have. Don't take me for a fool. At first, I spent days on my knees begging God to let me in, but it never happened. Finally, I decided to start questioning those who come back."

"And?" Caleb asked.

"They all say it's wonderful. Some have even been to higher levels. That's not the issue. Why can I not enter? Every time I've tried, fear takes a grip on me and I'm immobilized. I've been on my knees for days and watched hundreds pass by, some crying, some desperate, some with a smile on their face."

"I don't want to sound as if I'm downplaying your problems, Dr. Kendrick," Chen said, slowly. "But I think you need to take a vacation from this place. You need to travel. You need to get away from here for a while where you can think more clearly. Here, there are too many distractions."

"But I love this place." the professor whispered as he turned back to the window and watched the street below.

"I know you do," Chen said.

"Love is my weakness," the professor said, wistfully.

"Ah, Doctor, love can only be a weakness if you love the wrong things," Chen said as he glanced over to Caleb.

The professor didn't respond.

Caleb nodded toward the door. They both quietly rose and left the professor looking out the window.

"That is one confused man," Chen said as they walked out of the building.

"Remember the Spanish guy at the cafe in Havana? Said he'd been a priest. Said he wouldn't cut his beard till he was ready to walk right in. What was his name? Juan Marco, something," Caleb asked.

Chen sighed. "Yeah, he sounds just like Juan Marco."

Jake and Kunetzov were not at the corner they'd picked for the rendezvous, so Caleb and Chen decided to check out the market a block away since they were a little early leaving the professor's office.

"I suppose the comfy bed is out of the question now," Caleb said.

"There must be a motel or something nearby. Let's ask around," Chen waved toward the crowd they'd wandered into.

The stalls lined two sides of a street set aside for foot traffic. There was a coffee shop or snack bar every fifty feet. The rest were oriented toward clothes or trinkets with emblems embossed on them bragging that they'd been to the tower. As they ambled around the clutter of shops Chen stopped and beckoned Caleb over.

"I've been listening to that woman over there." Chen indicated a middle-aged woman sitting at a table in conversation with two others.

"What are they talking about?" Caleb asked.

"She's trying to convince the two others to take the walk."

Intrigued, they waited for the two others to leave, then Caleb stepped forward. "Pardon, Ma'am. My friend, here, overheard a little of what you were saying. Could we have a few minutes of your time?"

The woman smiled and waved to the two vacant chairs. The street was crowded with people packed in milling about.

"How may I help you?" she asked as they pulled their chairs close.

"We need advice about going into the tower," Caleb said.

"Are you in Eden City for that purpose or are you just curious?"

Caleb said carefully, "We intend to go in, but I feel like we should prepare or something."

"Preparing is the easy part," she said. "Being prepared is the hard part."

"Sorry, I didn't quite get that," Caleb said.

"You're either ready or you're not. If you're ready, preparation is easy. You need to do nothing but move your feet. Getting to that spiritual place where you can let everything go and walk forward is the hard part."

"But should I take food or extra clothes? Do I need to wait for something, a signal or something?"

"The woman leaned forward. "That's interesting. Why would you wait for a signal?"

"To, you know, make sure the time is right."

The woman paused, looking thoughtful. "You're different from most who I talk with. Most want to know if they're worthy. They're looking for someone to tell them it's okay. You seem to have a more practical approach like it's part of your job."

"I guess I'm a practical kind of guy."

"You're more than that. I can tell. You're a man on a quest. Am I wrong?"

Chen interjected, "What do you mean by 'quest'?"

"A quest is a journey one takes to right a certain wrong or gain a certain insight. Something like that."

Caleb sighed. Then he whispered across the narrow table, "Look, don't say anything out loud, but back in my village an angel showed up and told me to go all the way up there. I've got a meeting with the big man."

The woman grinned, "I've been waiting for you. You must be Caleb of Savannah."

"You know about me?"

"Sure. Your instinct was right. You need to wait two days before you step into Eden—the real one. Someone is coming here to meet you."

Caleb straightened in his seat. "Is it Anna?"

"Sorry, I don't know who it is."

He looked at Chen. "It must be Anna. I can't think of anyone else."

Chen asked, "Madam, how did you come by this information?"

"It's good you asked. Most people just assume the Lord told me."

"Did you get a visit from an angel?"

"No, the Lord told me. In a dream. My dreams always come true, or I don't dream at all."

"Anything else in your dream gives you any hints about the person?" Caleb asked.

"Ah, let me think. I'm not sure how much is the Lord and how much is my mind. When I sit on these dreams too long, I get a little confused about it. I think it may be a woman."

"Why a woman?" Caleb sat forward.

"She likes to wear yellow."

Caleb slapped his fist into his palm. "That's Anna. She almost always wore some yellow."

"So, are you going to take the walk?" the prophetess asked.

Caleb's brows rose. "I assumed I would. Is there another way?"

"Sure, you could take one of those flying balls, the way some of the angels get around."

"I haven't seen one of those yet," Caleb answered, turning to Chen. "Have you?"

"Yeah, a few times. They make a humming sound as they fly over."

"I haven't been told otherwise, so I'm assuming I'll be going in at the entrance here."

"What about your friend here and Anna?"

Caleb leaned back slightly abashed. "I haven't even thought about it. I assumed Chen and Jake would go at least part of the way up there with me. Anna, too. Captain Newton told me she's been called, too."

"I plan on going as far as they let me," Chen said. "If I can."

"I'll ask Jake—heck, and Kunetzov if he wants to go with us."

When they got to the park, at the corner across from the university, Jake and Kunetzov were already there.

"We need to wait 'til day after tomorrow," Caleb told the men after they met up.

"Why? The professor gonna set us up for a few days?" Jake asked.

"Not the way the meeting went down," Caleb said. "But we met a woman, later, who knew who we were. She said someone's gonna meet us here the day after tomorrow. I think it's Anna, my friend from Paradise."

"Okay, so we can check out the city some more. I spent a lot of time on my hillside waiting for you guys, you know. I get bored easily," Kunetzov said.

"Yeah, you can tell us how it went with the professor," Jake said.

"Okay Colonel," Caleb said, to Kunetzov. "You know this city better than we do. But first, we need to clear something up. I intend to go all the way to the top. I've got a meeting with the king, and nothing's going to stop me, especially myself. And Anna's going with me. Chen says he wants to go. How about you, Jake and you, Colonel?"

Kunetzov shrugged. "I'm not a colonel anymore, guys. Not really a Russian, either. That's just my way of making theater. I've changed too much now." He paused. "I tried to go through the entrance once and it didn't happen. I'm not sure I'm capable of it."

Chen asked, "What did you learn during those years waiting on that hill if not to assess your relationship with the Lord? We intend to get there. We've made up our minds. That's what it is. A decision to do it regardless of the discomfort."

"Well said, Chen." Caleb added, "You haven't answered the question. Do you want to sit here all comfortable for a thousand years or do you want to take a chance and find out what's up there, or even out there? You know this tower goes past the atmosphere. I, for one, want to see everything. And I have a hundred questions ready for Jesus when we meet. We want you to go with us and give it your best shot at *your* destiny."

"Well. Can this old Russian colonel change his stripes? I suppose there's only one way to find out."

Jake clapped him on the back. "Alright! We three are now four, soon to be five when Anna gets here. Meanwhile, we have today and tomorrow to look around. Lead the way...ah, kunetzov, what's your full name anyway?"

Kunetzov snorted, "You couldn't say all of it if I told you. My comrades call me 'Boris.'"

Caleb held his hands wide. "Alright, Boris, lead the way."

Boris Kunetzov led them north away from the tower, and up the wide avenue. They chatted about the architecture and occasional changes he noticed. An electric car hummed past. "Fifty years ago, when I was last here, there were no electric cars. Most people didn't even have electricity in their homes."

"How'd they get around, then?" Chen asked.

"Walked or rode trolleys pulled by horses, mostly."

"I wonder what the horses thought about that?" Caleb said.

"I think horses are getting smarter every year," Boris said. "They were basically okay with helping us fifty years ago, but I knew a change was coming. Even back then there were a few defections, you know, horses not reporting for work, going wild, doing their own thing. Some came back because they liked hanging around with humans. They were not as taken-for-granted after that."

"What about other animals?"

"You can find pigs, cows, and other farm animals on farms all over, but we don't eat them anymore. That would be cruel. But if they want to hang out with humans, they need to figure out a way to be useful. Pigs are good at digging roots up. Chickens and geese remove bugs from crops. That sort of thing. It all works out."

As they crossed the street, a bus passed them and came to a stop a block away. Attached to the building was a sign with "Bus Stop" printed on it in red blocky letters.

"That's new," Boris said. "Public transportation is now electric, too."

"That bus looks like it's from out of town," Caleb said. He pointed to the marquee printed above the grill. "Evidently it's from Damascus. If Anna is coming from the north, this might be a good place to meet her. Let's check here day after tomorrow."

CHAPTER SIXTEEN

When Anna's bus entered Beirut, traffic had slowed to a crawl. Outside the bus window, pedestrians carried small signs welcoming some dignitary or other. A crowd filled the street for a few blocks in both directions till the bus passed through. When they got to the station, a nondescript building with a sign outside, the crowd had dissipated, and traffic returned to seeming normality.

Anna roused herself. "I wonder who the visitor is?" she asked Sandon sitting a seat over.

"We'll find out shortly, I think." Sandon pointed to the bus station. A sign had been hung by the entrance like the ones the crowd had carried.

The bus pulled to a stop, and they got out and stretched the kinks out.

"I'm getting hungry," Oscar said, looking away down the street for cafes.

Helen hitched her shoulder bag up higher. "Me. too." She turned to Sandon. "Okay if we check out the local food?"

Sandon said, "Sure, come on. My treat." He led them up the street toward downtown.

They found a cafe with outside tables. Two patrons sat at a table talking animatedly. A young woman leaned close to the other, waving her arms in excitement.

Anna and the others chose a table and sat.

The cafe, located at the corner of two streets, was blocked off for foot traffic only and served traditional Lebanese fare of which Anna was partial to. They ordered black coffee with bread and a shallow bowl with olive oil and spices mixed together.

Sandon broke a hunk of bread off the loaf and held it up. "Thank you, Lord of all," he said and dipped it in the olive oil and swirled it around to pick up some of the spices.

Oscar did the same, followed by the others.

A few minutes later, after they all had a few bites, Anna asked, "Sandon, what's our plan for the next few days?"

"I'd like to hang around here for a day, if it's alright with you guys," Helen interrupted. She indicated the two women at the nearby table. "Something interesting is going on."

"Yeah, I wonder who's visiting?" Oscar said.

Anna waved to the woman who was talking. "Excuse me, what's all the excitement about?"

The woman stopped her hand waving and turned in her seat. "You haven't heard?"

Oscar finished chewing. "We just got here."

The woman laughed. "Brother Paul is coming through here. He's recreating his journeys. He'll be here in a few hours."

Oscar frowned, turning to Sandon.

"She means the Apostle Paul," Sandon said.

Chewing quickly, Oscar said, "We need to see this. I've wanted to see him for a long time. I've got a zillion questions."

Sandon shrugged, "Why not? But there'll be a big crowd. We can…" Sandon paused for a moment with an unfocused stare, then looked back at his friends. "We have a change of plans. We won't be able to stay. We must finish our meal and get a bus to Nazareth."

Anna stopped eating. "What's in Nazareth?"

Sandon said, "Caleb is waiting for us in Eden City. But first, we need to go to Nazareth and get his parents. They will be going with us to meet him."

"What about Paul?" Oscar asked.

"You'll have another opportunity," Sandon assured him. "Anyway, there will be many in the tower who can answer your questions."

An hour later their bus pulled away and picked up speed. Knowing Caleb was so close, Anna had little trouble adjusting to the speed they traveled.

The trip to Nazareth was uneventful aside from the increased vehicle traffic and prevalence of electric lights in towns they passed through. Population levels seemed to be getting denser. More people were out on sidewalks going about their day. Anna saw a few children sitting with a matron in a small street-side park. A small van passed them, the logo on the side read, "Stan's battery and electric maintenance."

When the bus pulled into Nazareth, the sun had passed over the horizon, but it was still day as far as the residents of New Jerusalem were concerned. Stores were still open, people shopped, cafes were still busy.

They got off the bus a few blocks from the bus station. Sandon stepped to the sidewalk and waited for the others to gather close. "I know where they live. It's only a ten-minute walk."

Like most villages and small towns within the walls of New Jerusalem, Nazareth was well kept and manicured. Flowers grew along the streets kept by the citizens. The street was clean in spite of the dogs and cats roaming around or lounging about waiting for a pet and soothing words or a handout. When the electric service was reinstituted, the townsfolk decided to bury all the cables, so now, there were no poles rising above the streets and no wires running overhead.

They walked away from the corner downhill along the street. Anna sidled up close to Sandon. "Does Caleb's parents know we're coming?"

"I don't know. Probably not," Sandon said.

"Do they know Caleb is here, in heaven?"

"No, they have been told only that he is among the redeemed. They know they'll see him when the time is right."

"Okay. So, do they know about me?"

Sandon glanced down to Anna. "They'll like you. What's not to like, eh?"

Anna kept walking. "I don't know why I'm nervous. I've been meaning to look them up for years, but never got around to it."

They came to a narrow street leading back into an old part of the town, then to an alley ending at a small stone courtyard. Peering through the waist high gate, they saw a man standing before a head-high granite block chipping away with a chisel and hammer. Twenty feet away was the entrance to their home, a two-story stone structure built against a neighboring home. A trellis had been erected at the entrance and a woman dressed in a long skirt and loose white blouse was carefully twisting grapevines around it.

Sandon nudged Anna with his elbow. She stepped close to the gate, glancing quickly side to side, and called out, "Hello, friends."

The woman turned her head, registering the presence of others, and pulled her hands away from the vines. The man lowered the chisel and hammer and approached the gate.

"Hello, welcome to our home. Come in," he said, opening the gate and waving them inside. "Come in. Come in. Are you thirsty? We have tea and coffee and water, of course."

Sandon urged Anna forward.

Anna murmured, "Thank you, but we don't plan on staying long."

"I'm Daniel Carson and this is Beatrice. To what do we owe the visit?" the sculptor asked as he led them across the courtyard and to a wrought-iron table and chairs.

"We, ah, have news," Anna said.

"Oh?" The man said as he turned at the sound of his wife stepping outside with a tray and drinks.

Helen and Oscar found a chair and sat.

Sandon, preferring to stand, got to the point. "Your son, Caleb, is reborn. He is on his way to the tower."

The woman paused at the door, looking at the man. He glanced at her and back to Sandon and Anna. "And you are?"

Anna said, "I'm Anna Hudson." She indicated the others. "These are my friends, Helen and Oscar. This is Sandon, an angel of the Lord."

"Oh, thank you, Jesus." Beatrice set the platter down on the table and went to Daniel and hugged him. She turned to them. "We've been waiting years." She hugged Sandon and Anna.

Wiping away tears, she said, "Where is he? Is he on his way here?"

"No ma'am," Sandon said. "We are sent here to take you to him."

"Is everything okay?" Daniel asked. "I've not heard of a messenger announcing the arrival of one of the redeemed." Beatrice put her arm around Daniel.

Sandon smiled, holding his palms up. "All is well. This is a special circumstance."

"Where is he now?" Beatrice asked.

"He's in Eden City, waiting for Anna to arrive. He does not know you are coming with us."

"Pardon my questions, Sandon, but this is very unusual. You say he's not in trouble? What is this special circumstance?"

"I'd like some water, please," Helen blurted out.

Beatrice looked dismayed. "Oh, I'm so sorry. Here, let's all sit. This is all happening too fast." She passed the water around and stepped back inside to bring out a tray of snacks. Daniel brought more chairs outside.

After everyone had been served, they settled down to talk.

Anna asked, "How long have you been here?"

Beatrice took her partner's hand. "We were married for eighteen years and were reborn about the same time. I arrived in France and Daniel in Vietnam. We found each other about a year later and traveled around for about ten years and then settled here. We've been living in this same house for forty years. I've often wondered what was taking Caleb so long to arrive. I always knew he was redeemed. I knew the Lord Jesus answered my prayers."

Daniel interjected, "We figured we'd live close to the tower. We'd planned on going in soon, but never got around to visiting." He took a deep breath. "Okay, we're sitting. Let's hear it."

"Anna and Caleb are both called to the throne," Sandon said.

Beatrice put her hand to her mouth.

Daniel frowned.

Anna said, "A few months ago I was approached by a messenger. He arrived on one of those flying globes. He told me I needed to go to the tower and present myself to the Lord. It scared me so much. I was just barely getting comfortable with the idea of going into the tower to see the garden, but this was way outside my plans."

"Do you know why you and Caleb were called?" Beatrice asked.

Anna shook her head. "I have no idea."

Daniel said, "I died when Caleb was ten. Beatrice knew little of what he did after he left the army. Did he join the ministry later?"

Sandon said, "No. In fact, he did the opposite. Caleb became a mercenary and captained a company of soldiers till he died from a mortar shell, he, and some of his men. Then he met Anna in Paradise.

"The Lord's ways are a mystery, often even to me and my fellows. But he always has a plan. Caleb and Anna can be a part of His plan if they are willing."

Anna looked around at her friends and new acquaintances. "I'm willing. If only I knew what I'm supposed to do."

CHAPTER SEVENTEEN

The next day, after a fitful sleep, Caleb woke to light streaming in a window. They had found a couple of rooms for the night and woke early the next morning. Thirty minutes later they were having breakfast at a cafe a block away and planning their day.

"So, what do we do for now?" Jake had buttered a piece of dark bread and was looking at other tables for something sweet to put on it.

The waitress stopped. "Can I help you?"

"Do you have jelly or jam?" Jake asked.

The waitress nodded and came back a few seconds with a small ceramic pot filled with red jam.

Caleb waited as the waitress served Jake and walked away.

He considered the question. "You know, when I see that huge opening in the tower going into the dark interior, I keep asking myself the usual questions, like what I need to pack and for how long. That guy we saw run into the entrance the other day seemed to be carrying nothing except the clothes he had on. I'd rather be prepared for anything I'm supposed to be responsible for."

"We know the trees have fruit on them," Chen offered.

"Yeah, we won't starve." Boris pulled the pot of jam closer and tasted it. "Tastes Russian," he said and pushed it back to Jake.

Jake looked at Boris and the big blob of jam on his bread and said nothing.

Caleb said, "I think we should split up and meet back here at dinner time, say around seven. I want any information you can get on what it's like inside, especially from people who have already been in there. If you find someone who has been to higher levels, I'd want to meet them, if possible. Boris, want to pick a direction?"

"Sure, I'll go north."

Jake lifted a hand, "West."

"I'm thinking about going back to the university. Maybe I can get the professor to talk with me again. That would leave the east for you, Chen."

Chen nodded and sat back; his breakfast finished.

Ten minutes later, Caleb was walking to the university. Getting near the bazaar, he stopped to see if the prophetess was still there. She was nowhere to be seen, but as he was leaving the narrow street of vendors, he noticed two young men and a middle-aged man sitting at a table with thick bound books open before them.

"Morning, would you men know if the professor might be in his office?" Caleb pointed to the street past the huge stone columns to the third floor of the building there.

The youngest of the three said, "He's usually not at his office yet. I think he's still teaching a class. He runs over sometimes."

"Ah, I see. Then I suppose I need to kill a little time. What are those books? I haven't seen many books like those since I arrived."

The same student replied, "These are copies of the Holy Book of The Tower."

"Never heard of that one. Is it one of your textbooks or just some easy reading?"

The older man laughed. "This is the only book aside from the ancient scriptures that first year student's study."

Curious, Caleb asked, "I see. Ah, can you give me a general synopsis?"

"Not easily. It's very complex."

"I've got time," Caleb said, pulled a chair closer, and sat down.

"Well, I, ah, let's see, it starts with a summary of the War Counsel of Heaven and Battle of Satan's Defeat. Then there are fifty chapters of the Millennial Prophets. After that, the Poem of the Garden, and the Seven Hundred Steps of Perfection. Of course, you can't take much of it literally. It wouldn't make any sense."

"What wouldn't make sense? What's a good example?"

"In the Seven Hundred Steps it says you must ascend a staircase to reach godly wisdom and each one is like a mile high. Then later it says God's throne is guarded by beasts made of the stone of the world and they have men's faces and stand thirty-six feet in height. That's just a few. They are obviously to be taken allegorically. Otherwise, it just wouldn't fit with the most trusted theories."

The quiet one across from Caleb said, "Forgive Brother Clarence. He forgets one of our most important precepts at the university is to let each reader gain what he can from the text, on his own, first before going to the next level of instruction."

Caleb immediately wanted to get a copy of the text. "Is there a store I can purchase one of these books?"

"Sure, But they're always behind on orders. The university owns the presses and guarantees accuracy, though."

"I'll go by and put in an order then. Where would the store be?"

It turned out the store was located behind the second building of the university by transient quarters, where the monks lived. Caleb walked around back and stepped into the familiar smell of paper and ink. Shelves lined the walls packed with hardbound books of many shapes and sizes. Behind a counter near the back wall, a monk sat with eyes closed. As Caleb walked past the shelves, he noticed that, although the monk's eyes were closed, his lips moved imperceptibly.

Caleb coughed. The monk's eyes opened, and he smiled. "Welcome friend. How may I be of service?"

"I'd like to purchase a copy of the Book of the Tower."

"I see. We only have eight copies here, but they are all paid for and awaiting pick up. There is a three week wait. Can you wait?"

"Not really," Caleb said. "I'll be leaving in a few days."

"I'm sorry. You can read a copy in the library here on campus. Perhaps you can make do till a copy becomes available?"

Caleb nodded. "Alright, thanks." He walked out of the store, then stopped and went back inside. When he reached the counter he asked, "Would you have portions of the book printed separately."

The monk looked down, thinking. "Perhaps. I'll go in back and check." He came back out with three small, but thick books.

He put the three books on the counter and turned them so Caleb could see the covers.

As Caleb looked down at them, he could only make out letters in another language. "I'm sorry. What language are these in? I only read English." He flipped one of the books open and stared at the pages. "I can't read them. Can you?"

The monk stared at him in surprise, "Of course, I've been a student here for thirty-eight years. I have most of these memorized."

"Ah, sorry. No offense. There are only three books here. Which ones are missing?"

The monk put the three books side by side. "The War Counsel of Heaven is missing. So you would start with the Battle of Satan's defeat. Sorry, there is no commentary with any of these. Then the

Millennial Prophets and the Seven-Hundred Steps. The Poems of the Garden, my personal favorite is missing. Sorry."

"That's okay. I'll take these. How much?"

"I'll just charge you as if they were part of one book since you will not have a commentary to help you decipher them. That would be one gold piece."

Caleb paid him and left with the three books under one arm. He went straight to a seat in the park and sat down to make out from them what he could. He planned on looking over the books first, then going to the library and finding a student to help him.

Opening the first book, he put a finger on the page and scanned down. He could tell when a subject changed. The chapters were numbered. He couldn't even read the numbers, but he could figure that out eventually. He skimmed through quickly by flipping the pages, then went back to the front and settled in to scan for patterns. He knew those two words in the title were Satan and defeat, but after half an hour closed his eyes and closed the book.

"Lord, I'll never get anywhere like this. I need serious help." He felt a breeze across his forehead and opened his eyes to see a branch close by swaying in the wind. Sitting back, he picked up the Seven Hundred Steps and held it in his lap as he watched people walk past. He glanced down at the title again. This time it was clearly legible and understandable. He stared at it a moment, then quickly set it aside to pick up the Battle of Satan's Defeat and opened it to see clear and precise text, the meaning popping out at him.

As if pulled by an unseen hand the words drew him in, the meaning exact, as he read of Satan's grand strategy, his overplayed hand, his ego too large to use his forces effectively. He read of the gathered angels waiting in high ranks arching across the sky, blotting out the sun. He read of ten thousand rockets rising from the earth ready to unleash nuclear fire and he felt as if he heard the words, "It

Is Time", as the sky disappeared in nuclear fire. And as the sky cleared, Michael, riding a round white platform inscribed with the words of the holy prophets and the names of the apostles, sailed down through clearing sky to root Satan and his followers from their underground bunkers. Following him were ten thousand times ten thousand.

Caleb saw Satan's strategy clearly and knew immediately he could not possibly win. Almost all his military power was placed in the missiles. He knew, sadly, the war would degenerate into pulling the people of earth into the battle as they manned their warships, planes, and tanks. Billions would die.

Billions did die. Caleb shook himself and leaned back to rest his eyes. He had two pages left. He read them and saw the rest of the war only lasted another hour before the generals gave up, powered down, and left Satan and his lieutenants to fight it out alone against a foe too powerful to even imagine. At the end, the last battle of the war took place in Israel as scripture said over three thousand years before.

An hour had passed as he read, so Caleb, knowing he had the rest of the day, stretched, and opened the Seven Hundred Steps and began.

Caleb was sitting at their table when the others arrived from their investigations later in the evening. The three books sat on the table along with Caleb's glass of beer.

Chen was the first to arrive, nodding at him as he took a seat and motioned to the bar for a drink. A few minutes after he sat, Jake walked in with a dark little woman following closely behind.

"Boss, you'll want to talk to this little lady," Jake said, as he ushered the newcomer to the table and sat her next to Caleb.

"That's good news." Caleb nodded his head in greeting. "Let's wait for Boris to get here." A few minutes later Boris walked in, clean shaven and smiling.

At first, Jake stared at him frowning, then started clapping his hands. "Dang it. I didn't think you were gonna do it," Jake said.

Boris pulled up a chair and sat. "Who's the new person?"

"This is Reba Abraham, of Wheaton Illinois. She's been in the tower," Jake announced.

Caleb raised a hand. Attention turned to him. "Now that we're all here let's all make a report. Chen, let's start with you."

Chen said, "I headed east, walked all the way to the edge of town, about five miles. I saw nothing special, except for new construction. Three new homes going up. Seemed to be modern era stuff. Talked with some of the construction people. They were all fairly new to New Jerusalem. Met more interesting people on the way back. Nobody that's been in the tower."

Caleb turned to Boris.

"I walked about two miles north. Met nobody that's been to the Tower, so I figured I'd ask some local businessmen if they knew someone. Ended up at a barber. Left without the beard. That's it."

Caleb turned to Jake.

"This here's Reba. She has quite a story."

Caleb leaned back to see her better.

Reba looked around the group and sighed. "I'm not sure what I can tell you that wouldn't be better served by just going on in. Jake said you were once a military man. Well, you can't plan this like a campaign. I'm not sure how much I can tell you. You won't believe most of it anyway. I'm sure you'll act like you do, for my sake, but you won't believe till you see."

"Start with going in the entrance," Caleb said.

"Okay." Reba clasped her hands and stared into her lap for a moment. "As far as I know, I'm the only person who rebirthed in Eden City. Back then it was a small village nestled close to the entrance. I woke in a stone hut two blocks from here. That was almost three-hundred years ago."

She stopped and looked around the table. "I stayed in the village about ten days, then I walked into the tower. I didn't know what to expect except for what I had read in the Word: the Garden of Eden, the tree of life, peace, rest. I wanted all of that, had been looking forward to it for fifty years. After going in through the entrance, it took me a day to make it to the garden. I wasn't disappointed. One of the keepers introduced himself and explained how the garden was designed.

"We spent many months wandering around and laughing together. There are always lots of people and angels resting in the garden at any given time. At that time there were more angels than people, but I heard preparations were underway for a great many of the redeemed to come in soon.

"After a while, I felt the need to move on. I was rested. I felt so energetic and clearheaded. I had great questions and many unresolved personal issues. I knew I wasn't all I was supposed to be.

"There's a place in the garden special to me where the river is only thirty feet wide, and part of the great tree sits out in the middle of the water held up on roots like pylons. In some places, one can see underneath where water birds have nests and fish swim about. Sometimes the fruit, much like small peaches, drop to the water and the fish swallow them whole. After a month, I felt the need to be alone. That's the place I felt the most whole. That is where I prayed. That is where I decided to go deeper; I did that by going higher.

"The tower is a marvelous great structure. It's also a machine, much like a wondrous factory. I was told anything could be made there if one could describe it. Titanic and ancient forces are at work in the tower greater than the energies of any star.

"So, after much prayer, I traveled to the second level."

"How did you get there? Did you walk?" Chen asked.

"Yes, to get to the second level one must walk—and climb. There is a staircase a little over a mile high. I climbed it in about ten days, not because I was tired—I was well rested and in better physical condition than I had ever been before. It took me that long because of all the people I met. There were hundreds on it going up and down. There are places to rest along the way. I stopped often to join in discussions. Some people sat on the stairs and worshipped. Some prayed. Some just listened and smiled with eyes closed.

"Of course, I didn't know what to expect on the second level, but when I got there, I was met by a keeper who opened the great doors for me. Inside was a large town surrounded by forest and fields. All the animals talked, and the subject was usually about our Lord.

"I stayed there for three years, then went to the next level. In the end, I went to the twelfth level." She paused. "I think here would be a good place to stop. Some things are better discovered on your own.

"I spent fifty-two years in the tower, then the Lord commissioned me to leave the tower and to come down and travel the world of man, to be an example to the fainthearted."

They all sat quietly for a few minutes digesting Reba's amazing story.

Caleb asked, "Have you ever talked with the teachers at the university?"

"Oh, yes."

"I had a short conversation with Dr. Kendrick. He's an enigma," Caleb said.

"He's a coward," Reba said, flatly, patting the table with the palm of her hand. "I don't mean to be harsh, but that's the way it is. I don't know why he is and I'm not judging his moral character; he is what he is. We all have a need for maturing."

Caleb realized she was saying no more concerning the professor or the university. "I see. Thanks for sharing with us. As a side note, I wonder if you might have insight into my calling. You know my background. I've been trying to figure out what good I could possibly be for the Lord."

"Are you willing to learn?" Reba asked.

"Sure."

"Are you willing to take whatever job the Lord asks, even if it seems small?"

After a pause, Caleb said, "Yes, I believe I am."

"Then whatever it is will be something needful. Our Lord does everything for a reason. He is not frivolous with His people's lives. You will be doing something important, maybe saving lives, perhaps more important even than that."

"More important than saving lives?" Jake asked.

"You'll find out. Every level has a lesson. And at the top is our Lord's throne. I've heard of a few who have gone all the way."

"But climbing fifteen hundred miles seems impossible," Boris cut in.

"Ever hear about electricity, cars, planes, elevators?" Reba laughed.

"Ah, well, okay, I feel better now," Boris said with relief.

"You were reborn, here, in Eden City right near the entrance," Caleb said. "What was your life like before?"

Reba sobered. "I was a simple farmer's wife. My husband died young. We had no children, so I started an orphanage. Ran it till I was ninety-six."

A waitress stopped by the table. "Anybody here hungry?"

"Sure." Jake pulled out a gold piece. "I'm paying for everyone. How about a big platter of those funny shaped gyros with spanakopita and salad?"

"Okay, it'll be a few minutes." She walked away, jotting on a pad.

Chen leaned toward Reba. "You said there were lessons to be learned on each level. What did you learn on level two?"

Reba turned to Chen, "Have you ever had a pet? All the animals on level two are pets. Can you imagine if you could understand what they said? They all have a certain intelligence. They are limited by their place in the world, but God loves them, too. Level two teaches us to love the small and needy, the weak and imperfect. It is a necessary lesson to understand well before one goes any higher."

"So, everyone in the tower are vegetarians?" Boris guessed.

"Pretty much. There are fish and insects, though. They have no understanding and never will as far as I can tell."

Caleb laid his hand on the table by the books and drummed his fingers. "You're familiar with the Book of the Tower, I'm assuming."

"Yes, I've read it."

"Can you explain it to me?" Caleb asked.

Reba shrugged. "I can only tell you what I know. I've only been to the twelfth level. That's not very far—depending on your perspective, I suppose. It's mostly self-explanatory."

Caleb patted the books by his hands.

"I've been wondering about those," Jake said.

"Is one of those the Book of the Tower?" Boris asked.

Caleb nodded, then asked Boris, "Have you read it?"

"No, I never got around to it. I assumed it was a story like Pilgrim's Progress or Gulliver's Travels. Anyway, I only read Cyrillic and a little English."

"I don't have the whole book, only these three sections." Caleb passed the books around the table.

Chen took one and opened it. "What language is this?" Chen asked Reba.

"It's a mixture of lots of languages. It's what everyone speaks and writes past the tenth level," Reba said.

Chen flipped through the pages. "So, to live in the eleventh level I'd need to learn this language?"

"Not entirely. But as you go higher you will find less people who don't. It would be a good idea to learn it, now, if you can," Reba suggested.

Chen passed it along the table.

Jake took it and opened it. "Not anything I can read. Haven't they translated it to a few other languages?"

Reba said, "Sure, but this is a university town. They pride themselves on sticking with the original."

Jake closed the book and looked up at Caleb. "Okay, boss. Want to tell us about these?"

Caleb leaned forward and propped his elbows on the table. "I met a couple of students who told me about one of their textbooks, called the Book of the Tower. Then I went to the university bookstore. They didn't have one in stock, but I was able to get these three sections."

"Can you read them?" Chen asked.

"Not until I prayed about it." Caleb pointed to the book in Jake's hand. "That's the Seven Hundred Steps. You can guess what that's about." Caleb picked up the other two. "This is the Millennial Prophets. I only skimmed it. The other is the Battle of Satan's Defeat. You three will find it fascinating."

"I'm impressed," Reba said. "It took me three years to learn the language well enough to read them."

Caleb nodded. "It seems I'm on an accelerated schedule. I think the information in these books is something I'll need to know."

The ride to Eden City only took three hours. They left early as the sun came over the horizon. Anna no longer had a problem at all with the speed they were traveling. She wanted to go faster. They stopped a few times along the way to let travelers get on or off the bus.

Anna and Caleb's mother, Beatrice, took advantage of their time with Sandon to ask as many questions as they could.

"But what about Noah? After they left the ark, it seems like history just forgot about them," Beatrice said.

Sandon nodded. "I understand your frustration. Noah lived another three hundred years and ended up in Eastern Europe. He had a lot more children. By that time they'd changed his name to one of his titles. Many of his sons then became great men of legend. But it only takes a few hundred years for a fact to be considered a myth. He was buried in myth and the only accurate record was preserved by the sons of Abraham."

The bus passed by miles of fields covered in ripe grain ready for harvest. A couple of farm tractors were pulling large wagons with workers sitting on the back with their legs hanging over the side.

Helen pointed to them. "So, do they like working in the sun?"

"I think so," Sandon replied. "But in a hundred years there will be combines out there instead of field hands and simple tractors."

Sandon continued. "Anna, have you noticed the progress, the slow pace of technological advancement? Two hundred years ago there were no tractors. Two hundred years from now will be large combines instead of only small tractors. The world is starting over. Many people now on the new earth, in New Jerusalem and out in remote areas, understand higher technologies. Their knowledge will be welcome when it is time to make the first computers and antigravity devices. The growth never stops. New Jerusalem will never die and in ten-thousand years all the spaces within the walls will be living space for man. Mankind will continue to advance in both technology and in the spirit. They must advance together. It is the right way."

Oscar said, "Those globes we see the messengers flying around in. What about them?"

Sandon nodded." I'm not an expert on technology, but maybe, in a thousand years, mankind will be ready for them. There's no real hurry, is there?"

Oscar shrugged. "I suppose not."

The bus slowed as they entered a small town. They stopped at a bus stop and picked up a few passengers as others got off. The driver rose from the seat and announced a thirty-minute stop for a break.

Sandon said, "Anyone want to take a break?"

Nobody did. Anna asked, "So, what's the plan when we get to Eden City?"

Sandon said, "I've been in contact with my brothers. It's all arranged. We'll meet near the university. "

Helen leaned in close to Anna. "How you doing?"

"I'm nervous. It's been over twenty years since I saw Caleb. It may have been only months for him. I wonder if he's changed. Some people do so, dramatically, once they get here."

"We won't know till we get there, will we?" She squeezed Anna's arm.

"You're right. I need to have more faith. I know."

An hour later the bus reached Eden city and, in a few minutes, pulled to a stop at the bus station.

"So, this is Eden City," Helen said, looking out the bus window. "How far to the entrance?"

Sandon pointed south. "About ten blocks that way."

They gathered their belongings and got off the bus with Sandon leading.

It was approaching midday. People were out and about, strolling along the street, sitting outside open cafes. Businesses were busy with visitors from all around greater New Jerusalem. A young woman with a child walked by leading a large golden retriever.

They made their way past numerous shops and vendors, most selling items one might need to have if considering entering the tower.

They came to the main boulevard which had the high columns, on both sides of the street.

When the main building of the university came into view, Anna became even more nervous. She kept glancing around expecting Caleb and his friends to be waiting around the next building.

Sandon stopped at the corner where the university grounds started. They could see the park across the grounds and pedestrians going about their daily lives. "Let's wait here. There are benches at the park. We are to meet my brother there."

On entering the university park, they walked among manicured bushes and mown grass. They came upon a man sitting on a bench, legs crossed, reading a bulletin printed on flimsy cheap paper. His hair was grey and cut short. He smiled and rose to his feet when they approached.

"Greetings, brother and friends," he said, giving Sandon a quick hug, then putting out a hand to Oscar and the others.

"Lael, when did you get back?" Sandon said.

"About five hours ago. My mission didn't take as long as we had anticipated."

"Good to see you. This is Oscar, Helen, Anna, and Caleb's parents, Daniel and Beatrice."

Lael nodded with a smile. "You all seem to be in good health and good spirits. Do you feel the need to eat and be refreshed?"

"I'm getting a little hungry," Oscar said.

"Of course. You have been traveling. Let's find a place to sit and eat. We can discuss our next move."

They decided to visit the market a block away across the main boulevard with a view of the main university building. The market wasn't busy, and they quickly found a table on the sidewalk.

"So, what happened? I heard there was a major shakeup in the chain of command," Sandon said.

"Yes. So, there is. There have been promotions. You remember young Jonel. He got a new assignment. He's now commanding twenty. He's very excited."

"I'm not privy to military matters, usually," Sandon said, "But I can see changes. I'm just curious."

"Of course. These are exciting times."

"Have you been assigned to Caleb?" Sandon asked.

Lael glanced over to the others. "Yes, but not till later. I'll meet him and his men when the time is right."

"I see."

Anna said, "I'm really not hungry. When can I meet Caleb?"

"Now, if you like."

"Now would be good," she said.

"Okay," Lael handed her the bulletin he had been reading and pointed to the front page where he had scribbled an address. "Two blocks away is the cafe where Caleb and his men take lunch. They are there now. That is the address. Take Helen with you. The others might as well stay here, for now."

A few minutes later, Helen and Anna stood outside the cafe.

Helen fluffed Anna's hair a little. "You look presentable. Don't worry. Go on in. I'll be right beside you."

Anna pushed open the door and stepped into a dim room with tables scattered about. Only a few tables were occupied. She saw at the back, four men at lunch in deep discussion. Caleb's back was to her. One of the men nudged Caleb and he turned in his chair. His eyes went wide, and he immediately stood and turned to her and stepped forward.

"What are you waiting for?" Helen pushed Anna gently.

Anna stepped the remaining few feet, put her arms around Caleb and her head against his chest saying nothing, and hugged him tightly. They hugged for a full minute, then, grinning, Caleb said, "I hope I didn't take too long."

Anna pulled away and looked up into his misty eyes. "I felt like you would never get here."

"I'm here now. We're together again and we have all the time we want."

"That sounds like my Caleb."

Jake, sitting on the other side of the table, stood. "So, this must be Anna."

They turned to him.

With his arm across her shoulder, Caleb announced, "Guys, this is Anna, that I told you a little about." Caleb glanced around the room. "Let's find two more chairs."

Anna sat next to Caleb, hip to hip, their fingers entwined under the table. Caleb asked, "Was your journey easy?"

Helen answered. "Easy enough. We walked from our village for a few days, then Anna's guardian met us on the road, and we walked for a few more weeks. Then we took a bus."

"It was so fast," Anna said.

"I imagine you would find it so. They had nothing like that in 400 B.C." Caleb paused and turned to Helen. "You said, 'guardian?'"

Anna answered. "My guardian angel met us on the road. His name is Sandon. Nice guy. He's been preparing me."

Caleb nodded. "I was told you had been called, like me. I hope we will to be working together."

"I think so, but I don't know what we're supposed to be doing."

"Me neither."

The others talked quietly among themselves while Caleb and Anna got reacquainted.

After a few minutes, Chen said, "We've been assuming our mission—Caleb's mission—will be military in nature. Have you been told differently?"

"No," Anna said, "but for you that would make sense, except there's no one to fight. For me, I can only speculate."

"We're speculating, too," Chen said.

Anna squeezed Caleb's hand under the table." I need to tell you something."

"Sure, what is it?"

"Your parents are in town. We stopped by their town and brought them with us."

Caleb's smile vanished. "Here, in Eden City?"

"Yes."

Caleb looked up to smiling faces.

Boris grinned. "I've been looking forward to this. I knew it would happen eventually."

Jake agreed. "Looks like we're moving. Ready to go, Boss?"

Caleb squeezed Anna's hand lightly, "Yes I am. Let's go. Anna, will you lead the way?"

CHAPTER EIGHTEEN

Sandon, Lael, Oscar, and Caleb's parents, Daniel, and Beatrice were waiting at the park by the stone bench. Caleb, walking arm in arm with Anna, paused when they approached the park and squeezing Anna's hand said a quick prayer, then they stepped around one of the buildings to see Sandon and Lael standing, facing each other in conversation. Daniel and Beatrice sat on the bench looking away out into the trees and hedges.

Caleb's friends and Helen decided to wait at the edge of the park and watch from a distance.

Caleb and Anna stepped forward and approached the bench. Beatrice saw him first, then Daniel.

Anna let go of Caleb's hand as Caleb stepped closer.

Beatrice, with tears of joy running down her face, rushed forward and wrapped her arms around Caleb, and hugged him tight.

"Oh, my son, what took you so long?"

In that moment Caleb was incapable of saying anything. He stood tall in his mother's embrace and held her, looking down at her brown hair and smooth arms. Then, he turned his eyes to his father whom he had not seen since he was a young boy.

His father nodded back with a sober smile, eyes shining.

Caleb saw a man, older, but clearly in his prime. He had never got the chance to know his father except as a young boy and, as he studied his father's face, some of the pain he'd felt as a child at his father's passing away briefly surfaced, only to be swept away by his mother's embrace and the sight of his father, solid and present, unchanged from his last memory.

After a moment Beatrice let go of Caleb and, taking his arm, turned to Daniel.

"We're all together again. Praise Jesus, our prayers are answered."

Daniel put out a hand. Caleb took it and they shook hands, staring into each other's eyes. Then Daniel stepped forward and pulled his son into a fierce hug.

As he stepped back, he patted Caleb on the shoulder, knowing they would have plenty of time to talk later.

Daniel cleared his throat. "We've heard interesting things about you on our way here."

"Yeah, I've been called." Caleb turned and took Anna's hand and tugged her forward. "Anna has been called also. We've got to present ourselves to the throne sometime soon. Not sure on the schedule, though."

Beatrice put a hand on Anna's arm. "Let's sit here. You can tell all about how you two met." They sat on the bench and began a conversation lasting into the evening.

The next morning Caleb and Anna woke to sparkling light shining through their room's window.

When Anna woke, Caleb was sitting on a cushioned chair watching her. "You're just as beautiful as I remember you. For me, it's only been a few months. For you, years. I'm sorry for taking so long." He paused for a moment, then continued, "I understand, now, why the Lord keeps back some of our memories till we're ready. If

I had remembered you when I woke, I would have been in such a rush to find you, I probably would have learned nothing."

"Sandon said you were being tested."

"Yes, it entailed watching my two friends die and come back alive and the other one was meeting an old nemesis. The first was about remembering who my strength comes from and the second was about forgiving an old grudge."

Anna sat up. "I began remembering you about ten years ago. I had good friends and things to do. I knew you'd find me eventually--in good time." She put her feet on the floor, walked across the small room, sat next to Caleb, and leaned her head on his shoulder. "Now we're back together."

Caleb kissed her on the top of her head. "Tell me about your village and your friends."

"My two best friends are Helen and Oscar. They were the ones who welcomed me back into the village when I was first rebirthed."

"The same village? That's unusual. You're the first I've heard of that happening."

"Yes. I was born into the same village twice, the first twenty-seven hundred years ago, the second twenty-one years ago. Helen found me and brought me straight to Oscar and they showed me around the village."

"What was it like?"

"I was a little shocked it seemed so wild. Trees were everywhere, not like in my first life. I was raised only a few miles away in my first life and knew the area well, but the only things I recognized were two old buildings from my time and the well in the village center. Everything else had changed. We discussed much of it already. You'll remember, eventually. I recognized Mount Meteora, of course, but little else."

"You're right. I don't remember yet. I like the sound of your voice, though. Tell me again."

"So, Helen and Oscar were walking me through the village, and I remembered there was a path leading down a hill to my home, but not only is there no sign of a path, but there were so many trees I couldn't even make out the hill. And later, the only sign I found of my home was a few stones—the threshold stone and the lintel for our front window. That was a little sad. I got to know the people over the years. I liked my new life better, learned how to read Greek, Aramaic, and Hebrew."

"I haven't been back home to Kansas, yet. I imagine it would be the same experience for me, except Kansas is as flat as a plate."

Anna took his hand. "I'm going to change the subject."

"Okay," Caleb said, knowing it would be a serious change.

"On the way here yesterday, Boris said something about the Book of Seven Hundred Steps. Is that one of the books on the table at the restaurant yesterday?"

"Yeah, just plain text, no commentary. And not the whole thing."

"I'm familiar with it. I've read it. Have you?"

Caleb nodded. "Yeah, I've read the parts I presently have."

Anna said, "I lay awake last night for a while thinking about what our situation is now. Something doesn't make sense to me. In the Poems of the Garden, there's a lot of talk about the upward journey, you know, the journey up the levels of the tower. It was designed to take a thousand years to reach the top. I suppose it would be for the average person. but I know a few people have already gotten there. We're at year two hundred ninety-nine since the Battle of Armageddon. Some have reached the top after only twenty or so years, which means they spent very little time on some levels or skipped levels completely."

They lapsed into a comfortable silence.

Caleb said, "I wonder how much of a hurry we're supposed to be in."

He leaned forward a little in his seat. "I've not read the Poems or the War Council of Heaven yet. But I do feel like we need to get a move on, though."

"Okay, so let's talk with the others and figure this out."

Caleb kissed her on the forehead. "Now that sounds like my Anna."

A minute later they heard a knock on their door. Anna stood and opened the door. Chen stood in the hallway. "We're meeting at the restaurant. We'll see you there."

Anna nodded and closed the door. "Are you ready to go?"

The others were waiting at the restaurant and already halfway through breakfast when Caleb and Anna arrived. Chen, Boris, and Jake sat on one side of a long table. Helen, Oscar, and Caleb's parents sat on the other. They had been talking animatedly—mostly Jake—when Caleb and Anna stepped inside and approached the table.

Helen, close to the end, pushed a chair away from the table and motioned for Anna to sit. Caleb sat next to Anna and held her hand under the table.

Caleb nodded to the others. "Anna and I have been considering our next move. We believe the Lord wishes for us to work together on something—no idea what. But I feel we need to get a move on. So, I say we leave for the garden right after this breakfast. Evidently, we don't need to pack anything special. Just take our usual gear we have with us now and whatever is back in our rooms."

Caleb stared down the table looking at both sides. "So, who's going with us?"

There was a moment of silence, then Chen and Oscar rose from their seats at the same time. They glanced at each other. Chen said. "We will."

Jake stood. "Me, too."

Boris sighed and stood up. "I've been thinking about this for a long time. Now's as good a time as any."

Caleb turned to his parents. "What are your plans? I don't know how long we'll be gone. Will you come with me at least part way?"

Daniel glanced toward his wife. "We've taken our time and waited, mainly for your arrival. We think the time is right. We're at peace about entering in."

Caleb nodded and looked at Helen and raised a brow.

Helen grinned. "There's no way you all are leaving me behind. I'm in, too."

Caleb slapped the table. "Good, because we're leaving as soon as we fill our bellies and collect our gear. Anna and I will meet everyone at the entrance." He paused. "By the way. Where's Sandon and Lael?"

Daniel spoke up. "They said they'd meet up with us in the garden."

Caleb nodded. "Well, okay. Let's eat."

Chapter Nineteen

When Caleb and Anna reached the main street, they paused at the street bazaar and grabbed a few things. Leaving the crowd there, they stepped onto the main boulevard. Across from them the tall building of the university rose like a side of a large ship with many windows facing the boulevard and the activity below. They walked out onto the stone pavement and faced the imposing doorway of the tower a hundred feet away.

Thirty feet wide, it rose seventy feet up and topped by a solid lintel jutting out from the facade. On the facade was engraved the names of the twelve apostles. On the wall, at the sides of the doorway, other names were written, but too small to be read from where they stood. They could see into the passage only as far as the light from outside allowed, perhaps fifty feet. Below, set into the threshold, a single stone was set even with the floor and crossed from one side to the other. It was a natural red and on it were more names beginning with Abraham, then listing all the prophets and ending with John the Baptist.

A small crowd had gathered at the entrance. Jake, Chen, Helen, and Oscar were already there and in deep conversation with Sandon.

"I thought you were already inside?" Anna said to Sandon, as they stepped close.

Caleb gave his friends a slap on the shoulder. "Who are all these people?" he asked, indicating the crowd nearby.

Sandon said, "The word has gotten around that two called ones were about to enter. I'm here because I changed my mind. I didn't want to miss the looks on your faces."

"I'll bet," Anna said.

Caleb studied the scene around him. It was not a moment he wanted to forget. They were close to the doorway now, only twenty feet from the red threshold. He could see inside only about seventy-five feet, then the passageway walls and ceiling became obscured in shadow. He turned around and studied the main boulevard. It ran arrow straight for miles within the growing city and receded north into the distance. On each side for the entire distance, every three-hundred feet the huge imposing stone pillars rose up into the sky a hundred feet, defining the avenue as a special place, a place where journeys begin and some journeys end.

On his right, Caleb saw where the bazaar spilled out onto the boulevard for a couple of blocks. People milled about. Many stood still, turned toward him and his friends, watching. The buildings rose up many floors, some rising higher than the columns. There was no traffic on the main street for five blocks, but further away was the usual traffic of electric cars and trucks and an occasional horse-drawn wagon.

On his left, the main building of the university took up an entire block. High up on the third floor a still figure stood close to the window facing out. Caleb recognized it as Dr. Kendrick. Turning to face that direction, Caleb lifted a hand in greetings, then waved to him to come down and join them. The figure stepped back away from the window and out of sight.

Caleb sighed as he turned back to his fellows.

"I guess he needs more time," Anna said, having heard the story last night.

"I suppose so. When he's ready, he's ready."

Anna touched his arm. "Your parents are here."

Caleb nodded to his father and gave his mother a hug as they stepped into their small crowd.

"Who are the others?" Daniel asked Caleb.

"I'm not sure. I guess they want to go in with us. We seem to be attracting interest."

"Some people need a little motivation. It helps to cross when accompanied by others," Sandon said.

They were all quiet for a moment. Anna looked up at Caleb.

Caleb squeezed her hand. Then loudly enough for everyone to hear, he asked, "Anyone here like to say a prayer before we go in?"

No one answered.

Caleb's mother, Beatrice, said, "Perhaps the prayers have all been said. Now would be the time for action."

"Okay, let's..."

"Wait!" A voice called out.

They all turned to see Dr. Kendrick running, robe billowing. Behind him, four other professors followed at a brisk trot. "Wait!"

A few seconds passed as the doctor came to a stop a few feet from Caleb and his friends, breathing heavily.

"I want to tell you something...before you go."

"Are you going with us?" someone in the crowd asked.

He waved his hands in the air in response. "I don't know why I'm here. I just need to say something."

"Okay," Caleb said and motioned for the crowd to be quiet.

The professor pointed at Caleb. "You know this is a one-way trip."

"Not so. Others have returned," a person in the crowd said.

"I don't mean that. I- I mean you'll never be the same. You'll change. You'll never be the same person again. You can't go back."

"Well, that's kind of the point," someone said.

"Sir," Another professor edged close. "We need you back at the university."

Beatrice stepped forward and looked the professor in the eye. "What does scripture say? 'Verily, I say to you, except a grain of wheat fall into the ground and die, it abides alone. But if it dies it will bring much fruit. He who loves this life will lose it, but he who hates his life in this world will keep it unto life eternal.'"

"Professor, come back with us." Two of the other professors took him by the arms.

"No!" He jerked free and stepped away from them. "No. I've been miserable for years. I've loved my place here. It has consumed me. It has stunted me."

He turned his eyes to the entrance and screamed, "Lord, forgive me!" as he lunged toward the entrance, peeling his robe free and leaving it lying on the floor of the passage as he raced out of sight into the shadow.

"Oh, my Lord Jesus. Praise Jesus and our Father." The crowd started chanting the words and began filing across the red line, the blood-red line of forgiveness, and as one, walked into a new life down the passageway.

"Let's go," Caleb said, wiping tears from his eyes.

In silence, they followed the others.

CHAPTER TWENTY

Once inside, the shadows of the passage quickly gave way to soft light coming from the walls. Caleb and his group had walked only a few hundred feet when the passage began to widen. As they continued, they saw murals painted on the passage walls from scenes of history.

"Is that Moses crossing the red sea?" Anna asked.

"Yes, it is," Sandon said.

They passed many murals depicting stories they were familiar with and by the time they came near to the end of the passage they had slowed down to study them. The others in the crowd had moved out of sight and the doctor was nowhere to be seen.

"What is this?" Caleb asked. Chen, Jake, and Boris had moved in close to see better.

Sandon said, "This is a depiction of Satan's last battle, where he was defeated. This will be the last mention of him within these walls for quite some time. You will come to pity him greatly, even though he deserved everything he got."

The mural showed a battle in the sky, very much how Caleb had imagined it as he read about it in the book of Seven Hundred Steps. The angels of God were arrayed across the sky and Satan had personally come out of hiding to direct the war. Missiles were rising up to meet the angels as blinding white rays of light streamed down to the earth to root out Satan's followers.

"Wow, that's powerful," Jake whispered in awe.

Sandon nodded, then said to Caleb, "There's a description of this in the Seven Hundred Steps, but I think you've already read it. Right?"

"Yeah, not so ancient history."

"I gotta get a copy of that in English," Jake remarked.

Sandon turned to Jake. "Given time, you'll read it in the original."

"I hope so," Jake said as they turned from the mural and continued down the passage which continued to widen till, near the end, they stood on a wide covered porch with steps descending to a park below.

In an arc across their view was a sight so magnificent no one was able to speak. Anna leaned against Caleb, tears welling up.

Chen dropped his pack and stood in awe. Daniel held Beatrice tight against his side with one hand over his mouth.

Oscar and Helen leaned against each other, mouths open.

Caleb stood stiffly, one hand on Anna's shoulder and the other clenched tight into a fist held against his chest.

Jake, with wide eyes and jaw hanging, said, "I never knew anything was this beautiful."

Before them, the view extended out for miles in a hundred shades of green. The roof of this ground floor must have been thousands of feet above, because the sky, bright and blue with streaks of silver clouds and gold beams extended as far as they could see. In the distance, large colorful birds flew across the sky and, in close, small birds flitted from tree to tree as they chittered and called. Also, in the far distance—perhaps ten miles--they could barely discern a structure rising above the trees, white stone reflecting light from above.

They stood under a low ceiling carved from wood, giving them shade and a sense of perspective. Fifty feet below, the steps ended, and low grass, manicured, lush, and green continued down a slight decline into a shaded forest of large broadleaf trees. A well-worn path began at the bottom step.

A short walk away, near the path, in the shade of the trees stood a shrine and around it a covered patio extended out to connect with fountains and round pools of clear blue water at different levels, each emptying into another till the last became a stream leading away into the forest.

In the stream, fish splashed as they moved from one pool to another. Long-legged birds lazily moved about. A dozen persons lounged on wicker or stone seats and watched as the birds came near to pluck morsels from their hands. Small mammals scurried among the trees and on the ground. Dogs, tails wagging, stopped and observed the new people at the top of the steps.

The air was crisp, clean, and energizing. A mist rose from the ground that hovered around the trees to dissipate in the soft breeze.

The more Caleb observed, the more life he saw. A mouse sat on a tree limb. An otter lounged in wet repose by a log. A parrot stared at them with a red circled eye. At the edge of the trees, a tall grey and white horse grazed on long grass. A foal skipped about her legs.

Not only was the sight beautiful, but the air hummed with expectancy. The trees seemed to encourage one to come within and rest. The animals and birds and fish invited one to come and play and learn.

After a few minutes of quiet observation, Sandon beckoned. "Come this way." He herded them over to the side of the porch where another path led down and out into the trees. At the end was a wide pool welling up from bedrock and flowing slowly away under overhanging limbs. Sandon led them to a stone dock where three boats sat in the water each big enough to accommodate them all.

"I'm to show you the centerpiece of this garden, then we must ascend. Let us embark."

Shaken and expectant, they all got in the boat and sat on the pillowed seats. The stream took them away into the forest.

For the next two hours, they cruised down the wide stream occasionally seeing people lying on the streambank or splashing in the water. Usually where people were there were also animals. It was easy to forget they were in the tower. The ceiling was high enough to be out of sight. The last wall they saw was the one inside the entrance.

Jake sat at the rear of the boat, fingers trailing in the water. He said to Sandon, "I've got to ask how big this place is. I know the tower is like fifty miles across, but how much space is in here? How far to the other side of this room?"

Sandon considered, "Not sure exactly. I get that question sometimes, but let's say about forty miles away to the far wall. It's different depending on which direction and where you would measure from. That's not my area of expertise. I'm sure you'd find someone who knows if you stay in here long enough. Perhaps if you ask one of the keepers. We'll meet them later at the great tree."

"That's something I'm looking forward to seeing," Oscar said.

A few minutes later the stream converged with another larger stream. Caleb had lost track of which direction they were going. The stream meandered so much that he was already lost.

The countryside they had passed so far was wild looking except for the few small structures they saw, but now the landscape took on a kept look. The trees were taller and neater and well-spaced. The shrubs grew in straight lines along the stream bank or receded away at angles as if separating areas for special purposes. They came around a bend and the great structure they'd seen from the porch hours ago perched on the bank and out into the stream. As they came closer, they saw that it was a shrine made of stone, many stories tall and covered in carvings of plants with murals of pleasant nature scenes in between. A porch surrounded the shrine on four sides and under the roof it was crowded with people.

They pulled up to the dock and tied off.

Sandon said, "Feel free to look around. We're not in a hurry right now."

Standing on the stone pier, Caleb called the group to gather around. "I don't know how long we'll be here. How about we meet at that spot over there," He pointed to a spot under the porch where a mural presented a scene of mountains and lakes. Tables and chairs were set up by it in the shade. "In ah, not sure how to measure time in here--say about two hours?"

"Sounds good." Jake tapped Chen and Boris on the shoulder, motioning for them to follow.

Oscar and Helen left together to look inside the shrine.

Caleb asked of Anna and his mother, "Any particular direction?"

"Yes, let's walk around the porch for a while. Find out what people are up to," Beatrice said.

Beatrice took Anna's arm and they walked away leaving Caleb and his father to follow.

This was the first time Caleb had a chance to be alone with his father. He had so many questions about his childhood and was unsure of his own memories. They walked in silence for a few minutes.

Caleb said, "You look the same as I remember, except for the clothes. In most of my memories, you were in jeans and tee shirt with a small calculator and pencil sticking out."

Daniel nodded. "Yeah, those were the days when I worked on my projects in the shed." He stopped at a mural and studied it a moment. "I was shocked to see how big you'd gotten. I think you took that from your mother's side of the family."

Caleb paused, thinking about which words would convey his feelings. "Memories of my childhood are mostly a blur. I was always outside building forts and carousing. I suppose there isn't much use in reminiscing, though. We're all back together. We have plenty of time to get to know each other."

"That's true, but know your mother had a lot of difficulties when I died, having to raise you by herself. Since we found each other again, we took the time to work through all those emotions. You'll need to do the same, eventually. When you're ready we can talk. I'm not going anywhere."

"I'm not sure I can say that. I don't know what the Lord has in store for me."

Daniel nodded. "I know. I'm sure He will give you the time you need."

They walked around the corner of the building and met Chen, Jake, and Boris.

"Anything interesting?" Caleb asked.

"Nah, guys playing chess and some other game," Jake said.

"Anyone see where Sandon went?" Caleb asked.

"Yeah, he's in there." Boris pointed at the open door to the interior of the building.

Caleb hooked a thumb at the doorway. "I'm going to wait here. If you guys want to look around, go for it. I need to talk with Sandon."

Daniel left with the others as they wandered away to explore. Caleb watched them walk away, then stepped through into a well-lit room. Chairs and couches sat against the wall. Two doors exited the room leading into other areas of the structure.

As he looked around, Sandon came out of one of the doors and raised a hand to Caleb. "Want to see something?"

Caleb walked over to Sandon. "Sure. Lots to learn here."

Sandon led him back through the door he'd just walked out of, turned down a hallway, and entered an office with a desk and chairs. Across from the desk, a screen three feet square was fixed to the wall.

Sandon walked around the desk and touched a few places on the flat glossy surface. The screen on the wall came alive.

Sandon looked up. "This bit of technology functions similarly to a computer but doesn't derive its usefulness from electronics."

Caleb looked at Sandon and lifted a brow.

Sandon chuckled. "I've spent thousands of years on earth as a guardian. Anna wasn't the first or last person I guarded. So, of course, I know all about electronics. In the tower, it's considered to be quite primitive, though."

"What does this do?"

"I thought you might want to see a map of the garden. Am I right?"

Caleb nodded and stepped closer. "What do I need to do?"

"Put your hand right here on the desk." Sandon pointed to a slightly raised square on the flat surface. "Put your hand on this spot and think of what you wish to see. At first, the whole map will appear. Then the desired place will draw close and expand as you wish it to."

Sandon stepped aside and turned the chair toward Caleb. "Might as well sit and get comfortable."

Caleb sat and pulled the chair close. Staring at the screen, he put his hand on the square. The screen immediately hazed out and returned with a vivid and detailed picture of the garden, like a view from a satellite. Details of the walls of the tower and supporting columns within were marked in red. Other details were marked in various colors.

"Okay, this is the garden," Caleb said out loud, "then this area here," and as he said the word the screen immediately expanded to show the entrance to the garden where they first stepped inside. It kept expanding till he saw the porch and shrine then drew the eye in close. The horse and foal were still there grazing. The horse's tail flicked, and the foal walked about.

"What?" Caleb said. "Is this live?"

"Yeah, it's live. What you see is happening now. All of the garden can be seen like this down to the veins on a blade of grass."

"Wow, I can see how useful this is," Caleb said.

"There are seventy shrines and each one has this device. This one is for office use, but there is one another here for general use. It's in our archive room."

Caleb took his hand off the square and turned to Sandon. The screen fuzzed out. "Why are you showing me this?"

Sandon waved at the wall. "Don't you want to see the holy Tree of Life?"

"Uh, sure." He put his hand back on the square and the map came up and immediately went to the center of the map.

He turned his eyes to Sandon. "You seem to understand people well."

"Yeah, I've had plenty of time to study humanity. I've been guardian to over forty people. Most were unique in some way. I could write a book, but it would probably be boring. Writing's not my specialty."

"Yeah, I know what you mean." Caleb turned back to the screen. The view swept down to float over the treetops then fly away to the side and descend to just above ground level. He saw people standing near the widest trunk he'd ever thought possible. The trunk was easily fifty feet in diameter and fifty feet high to the first branch. The main branches spread out twenty feet thick from the trunk and separated into smaller and smaller branches till the sky was blotted out for hundreds of yards in every direction. Pods hung from the branches, growing down to hang six feet from the ground. As he watched people plucked fruit of varying colors and walked away to find a place to sit and enjoy.

He panned the view around and saw that the tree was in the middle of a manicured park. There were thousands of people moving about, laughing, resting, and exploring. A wide stream ran nearby under the tree canopy. Many small boats rested at a stone dock with others arriving and departing.

Caleb removed his hand from the control pad. He turned to Sandon. "Any particular reason you wanted me to see this?"

"Yes, you're the bright one. We will not have time to see the tree in person, for now. Our schedule has changed a little. I thought you should at least see what it looks like. I figured you would be curious."

"Actually, I was and still am. But I'm more curious about my calling. When do we leave?"

"When Anna is ready. Perhaps she would like some time with this device, then we can leave immediately."

Sandon and Caleb found the others sitting at the tables near the mural. They all exchanged information, then Caleb took Anna to see the map and explore a bit.

After an hour at the desk, Anna took her hand off the pad. "That was so exhilarating. It's like I had wings."

"Good, I knew you'd like it. Now we need to find Sandon and tell him we're ready to go to our meeting."

Anna rubbed her hands together. "I'm nervous. Are you?"

"Sure, but I guess my curiosity dulls it a little. My guess is our meeting with the Lord will be at the top, fifteen hundred miles straight up. Now, that makes me nervous."

They found Sandon just outside the door. He'd been patiently waiting for them. He said, "You guys good to go?"

"Yeah, as ready as ever," Caleb said.

Sandon led them to the end of the hallway to a staircase and started up. They got out on the third floor to find Lael waiting for them. He stood by one of the large silver globes.

Lael, smiling, said, "You'll like this." He touched the globe and a door appeared on its side, sliding soundlessly into the craft's wall. "Hop in. We'll do a short tour first."

The four of them entered the truck-sized globe by walking up a thin metal ramp to stand together inside. Lael placed his hand on a pad protruding from the wall on a short stalk. The door closed, the walls went transparent, and the globe rose up to pass through an opening in the structure's roof. They rose upward for a few seconds, with no sense of movement, then quickly sped away from the shrine fifty feet above the treetops.

Lael announced, "We'll be passing above the holy tree at the center of the garden in a few seconds. The stone wall over there is an internal buttress for the tower. There are twelve of those." They passed over multiple small rivers and streams and over the old city of Jerusalem, still mostly in ruins, now home to a few souls, and saw evidence of small semi-permanent dwellings. All was green and lush, calm, and beautiful.

They slowed when they came to the far wall. A waterfall cascaded down from an unseen height. The wall appeared out of the spray.

They slowed to a crawl, passing through the spray, and landed on a platform against the wall poised a little above the treetops.

They got out and the globe sped away. A wide door in the wall appeared and they stepped into an elevator big enough for a hundred people.

Caleb and Anna stood in the cavernous elevator with Lael and Sandon, having left the others at the garden shrine. The shield and sword Caleb, Chen, and Jake had carried since the encounter on the beach lay on the floor at Caleb's feet. Caleb and Anna felt small, and they felt even smaller when one entire grey wall cleared to reveal the countryside below outside the tower. They saw the white block of buildings and the green and gold of cultivated fields and plains of grass, the blue of lakes, and dark green of forests all scattered about covering the flat plain as far as they could see. Caleb guessed they were already a thousand feet high and as the elevator began to pick up speed, Caleb felt it in his legs. Otherwise, there was no sense of movement except for the sight outside the tower. They rose upward, picked up more speed and the countryside began to recede away.

"At this rate, it shouldn't take us long to reach the top," he said to Lael.

"About twenty minutes, I've been told."

As they watched, low clouds obscured the view and quickly passed. Another series of clouds followed, passing by swiftly, then bright light from the distant sun shone and washed the inside of the elevator.

Caleb stepped closer to the clear wall and the vista below. The flat horizon extended for thousands of miles with greens and beiges interspersed with hazy clouds. Looking up, he saw brilliant stars shining down from a clear blue sky.

A few minutes later, the view darkened to a blue haze.

Caleb turned to Lael. "What is that?"

"Ice. We've reached the edge of the atmosphere. Ready yourself."

A few seconds later, they rose above the ice and the stars pierced the night with sharp clarity.

"Whoa," Caleb said as he reached out a hand back to Anna. She stepped forward and took it, standing close to him.

"That is so stark and clear," Anna gasped.

"I've seen a few clear night skies, but nothing like this," Caleb said, pulling Anna closer to the elevator's window. The Milky Way stretched across the sky. Caleb's heart swelled with the possibility of adventure.

As they watched, a glittering white craft many miles across and hundreds of miles long bisected the night, blotting out a thin section of stars. Smaller craft swarmed around it entering or exiting it from an opening like a white lit mouth. Wordless, Caleb, and Anna stared in wonder.

Lael asked, "Have you considered how angels get around?"

"Yeah."

"That is one of our ways," Lael said, pointing toward the craft many miles away.

"This is nothing like what I believed as a child," Anna said. "As a child I imagined angels flitting about the sky with bird wings attached to their backs and robes fluttering in the wind."

"Yet this is only your first time up here. This is a beginning for you. You have a body, which won't die and a God who will preserve justice. You have much to look forward to."

They stood in silence as they sped upward, still increasing in speed, while the night sky and stars rotated around them.

"We still have a thousand miles to go," Lael informed them.

After a moment, Anna turned to Sandon. "You're very quiet."

"This is my first time to ride an elevator with a view," Sandon replied.

"You've been on others, though. Right?"

"Sure, but this elevator is different. There are many, but this is the only one I know of that shows what's outside. This is new for me, too."

Anna smiled. "Oh, nice."

As they watched, the large craft receded below, and a new sight presented itself. Caleb looked upward as a yellow sphere moved by from the left to the right, passing out of sight.

"What was that?" Caleb asked.

"That is one of the Lord's orbiting habitats. There are twenty-four of them, each a home for one of the twenty-four judges that sit at the Lord God's feet."

As they rose, another habitat hove into view, this one with a reddish hue.

"They are ten miles across. I've been to one of them," Lael said.

A few minutes later another came into view. This habitat had a craft approaching it and another leaving. Caleb turned to Lael. "Something's not right. If they are orbiting the earth, they should be receding and moving away, not going that way." Caleb pointed to the right.

Lael nodded. "I was not clear. They are not orbiting earth. They orbit the tower. The tower is the center of all things earthly. They orbit below God's earthly throne. You'll see soon. But before you meet our Lord Jesus, there is someone who wishes to see you."

"Ah, someone else up here wants to see me?" Caleb lifted a brow.

"Yes, he is one of your ancestors. Your grandfather to be exact, but many times removed."

"What do I call him, 'Granddad'?"

"You can call him whatever you feel comfortable with, but 'Abraham' will do."

The elevator began to slow as Caleb and Anna stood by the window, shaken yet again.

Chen, Jake, and Boris watched as Caleb's parents hugged him and Anna then stepped back. Caleb and Anna followed Sandon through the door and disappeared.

Jake said, "Well, we don't know how long they'll be gone, so I think we might as well head on to the next attraction."

Oscar and Helen, who had been off exploring, walked inside the shrine. "What's up, everyone?" Helen asked.

Beatrice said, "They're gone to their meeting with the Lord. We might be waiting for a while."

"Any idea how long they'll take?" Oscar asked.

Daniel shrugged. "I have no idea, but if it's long, I'm sure they'll get word back to us."

"Okay, I say we might as well go exploring." Jake looked around at his friends.

Chen agreed. "Let's ask for directions and go find the tree where all of history started."

A few minutes later they all had gathered on the boat they arrived in and were floating with the current toward the center of the great garden.

The stream moved languidly. It was deep here, and the clear water allowed everyone to see to the bottom twenty feet below. Fish swam about and crayfish darted along the bottom. They turned a corner and passed a small crowd of people that had jumped in the water for a swim and waved as they passed.

The stream took them around another corner and the number of people present increased dramatically. A crowd of listeners sat on the grass or stood about, their attention on a tall man with long hair and bronze skin who paced about a makeshift stage waving his arms around and making faces. They could hear the laughter from the boat and as they passed by the man on the stage bowed to much clapping and stepped down. Another took his place and began singing and dancing.

Soon, another stream merged with theirs and it became a little wider. On the shore, on one side, a man and woman trimmed bushes with long bladed shears and piled the short trimmings in a two-wheeled barrow. On both sides of the stream, the general shape of the trees and bushes took on a decidedly manicured look. The trees were taller and wider with space underneath where one could see clearly between the trunks and much shaded space where light dappled the grass and thick green moss.

Before the vast bulk of the great tree came into view, they saw its fruit. Above, hanging out over the stream, long, thick branches spread high and wide, blotting out much of the light from above and shading the stream and bank on both sides far into the forest of other trees. Fruit of all colors dangled from long stems, reaching almost to the water in some places. Then they saw the trunk a hundred yards away seeming to be a wall of rough rock instead of wood and sap. They all stared in awe at the majestic height and girth of this ancient tree whose age spanned through all of mankind's history.

Their boat coasted close to a dock made of carved stone, solid and sturdy. Jake picked up the oars that lay in the bottom of the boat they'd not needed till now and directed them toward the dock. After tying off, they got out, staring in all directions.

It was fifty feet from the end of the dock to the bank and as they walked together under the shade of the giant tree, they encountered other people in awe as they were. Some were eating fruit as they passed by at a slow walk or lazed about among stone seats, eyes closed and smiling, in prayer, thinking, or even asleep.

"This has got to be the biggest tree in existence," Oscar said, looking up, craning his neck as he tried to see into the higher branches.

"I'd bet on it," Jake said. "So, who's going to try the fruit first?"

"Chen said, "I will", and stepped onto a bench to reach a red fruit hanging in bunches from a long stem, much like grapes, except bigger. He grabbed some and passed them around till all got one, then took the last for himself and took a bite.

Grinning, he said, "Very delicious."

After a few minutes, they had all eaten theirs and rinsed their hands in a water basin close at hand.

A series of paths had been designed around the trunk. They were inlaid with slabs of solid gold and edged with silver interlocked blocks, keeping the green moss in check. Statues of flowers, carved from white marble, squirted arcs of clear water across the path, over their heads, to land in marble basins on the other side.

The atmosphere under the tree was of contemplation and quiet discussion. The group didn't speak much. There was a lot to take in.

A few minutes later, they came to a keeper, dressed in a white robe and golden girdle around his waist. He sat on a bench and held quiet discussion with a small group of people who sat on the moss facing him.

They stopped and listened for a while before moving on. After two hours, they had circled the tree, and heard more discussions.

Boris said, "Did you hear what the keeper said about the old city of Jerusalem?"

Daniel, holding Beatrice's hand, nodded. "Yeah. I've wanted to see it for a while. I think it's only about five miles from here.

"It doesn't seem like it, but we're in something of a valley. This branch of the stream flows from the area near the old city. We can go visit it if you want. We can take the stream part way, maybe. Let's ask somebody."

Oscar said, "I think I'll stay here for a while. I've got questions."

"Me, too," Helen said.

Beatrice had been watching a teacher standing with his back to the broad trunk. He had a long black beard and wore a one-piece robe, cinched at the waist. A semicircle of listeners sat at his feet. Others had paused, in passing, to hear. She lifted her hand to a short woman walking by. "Ma'am, is that an angel or a man speaking over there?"

"You're new here, then? That is the prophet, Isaiah. He comes down here often to enjoy the garden."

Beatrice turned to the others. "I'm staying here for a while."

Daniel put an arm over her shoulders and spoke to the others. "We've got lots of questions, too."

A few minutes later, it was settled. Oscar, Helen, Beatrice, and Daniel would stay by the tree and Chen, Jake, and Boris would go to the old city and explore.

Chapter Twenty-One

The elevator began to slow, finally came to a stop and the wide door irised open to reveal a platform and a small valley receding into the distance. They stepped out onto the platform and surveyed the scene. The air was warm and dry. Trees were sparse and the ground was mostly flat under a bright sky. A silver globe floated down and landed near them. The doorway irised open in silent invitation.

Following Lael, they stepped in. The door slid closed, and the craft rose and headed out into open desert. Traveling close to the ground, Caleb saw even though they were in the desert, it was a healthy desert. A herd of camels meandered across the sand below them, double humps swaying. A fox stepped out from under a bush, its sharp eyes searching for prey. They crossed a river that rushed away into the distance. Soon they came to an oasis surrounded by high craggy hills on one side and orchards on the other. In the middle, a solitary, stone house, appearing very much like the hills, stood three stories tall, solid and grave, the roof covered with tan tile. Dogs scampered about while horses and camels wandered around the open ground or fed on hay at a feed stall mounted against a wall.

As the globe descended and landed near the front door, a matron stepped out and watched.

She smiled when she saw Lael, stepped close, and gave him a hug. "Good to see you again, Lael. How long has it been?"

"A few years. Seems like more." Lael turned and indicated Caleb and Anna. "This is Caleb and Anna, who have been called. Abraham wanted to meet them. Is he home?"

"Of course." Sarah turned and went inside. They followed her into the cool of the home and waited.

After a moment, a man entered the front room from a side corridor and approached them. His eyes, grey and wise, measured them as he stepped closer. He looked Caleb and Anna over, then turned to Lael. Speaking in Hebrew, he said, "Greetings, Lael." He added, "Have they received the gift?"

Lael nodded. "Caleb has received. Anna has not."

Abraham nodded and turned his eyes on Caleb. "My son, your appearance reminds me of my son Isaac." He paused. "I received word only a few hours ago of your calling and was curious about your nature. I can see you are a strong man. Our Lord has chosen well. You will do what is needed. I know little of your calling—for you, a better word would be, mission, I think. You are a man who does well when given a mission."

He turned his attention to Anna. "Do you understand my words?"

Anna nodded. "Yes, a little."

"Good. Where Caleb is weak, you will be strong. That is your mission." He smiled a broad smile. "Where are my manners? Let's retire to the back porch. It's cool at this early hour." He yelled, "Sara, would you please be so kind as to bring refreshment?"

They followed Abraham through the house to the back which opened onto a covered porch facing the arid hills.

They sat on the floor and leaned back into pillows. Sarah came from the house with two trays. She passed drinks around and lay the other tray down for them to try dates and other fruit.

Abraham lay back on an elbow, sipped his drink, and put it down. "Caleb, tell me of your life."

Caleb thought for a moment. "I was raised in America out in the Midwest, in Kansas. Joined the army at seventeen and made a career of it for a while. Then joined a private army."

"Private army, ah--for pay. I see. You were a soldier of fortune, then. Did you fight against evil, only?"

"I think so. We, ah, helped kings with neighbor problems. Guarded refugees. Helped take down a few warlords."

"Good. I'm proud to call you my grandson, even if far removed."

Sarah left and came back with another tray and sat beside Abraham. "So, did I miss anything?"

"Yes, Caleb rid the world of evil people for a living."

"Oh? Not bad. No wonder you were called." She sipped her drink.

"Ah," Anna raised a hand and put it back down. "You know something about our calling, don't you?"

"Very little," Sara said.

Caleb leaned forward. "Are you allowed to tell us anything about it?"

Abraham frowned. "My apologies. We may not. Our Lord wishes to tell you himself. Be aware, though. You both may be tested."

"This is very frustrating. I hope I don't go crazy before we find out," Caleb sighed.

"Not to change the subject, but can you tell us about you two?" Anna asked.

"We're in the Torah. You've read the Torah, yes?"

"Yeah, we've read it, but I want to know the stuff not said," Anna answered.

"Oh, that." Sarah sipped. "That would probably be mine to tell."

The next few hours Caleb and Anna relaxed in the company of another of God's chosen and learned something of the meaning of purpose.

Later, standing outside and looking out at the desert, Caleb said, "I was expecting you to be living in a palace, surrounded by people, not out here just the two of you."

Abraham laughed. "We are on vacation of sorts." After a moment of hesitation, he said, "When we first came here to this great city, we spent many years up there learning of our God's plan." He pointed upward. "We were a part of his council of twenty-four. We stood as judges for almost two hundred years, then we traveled a bit."

Anna said, "So you lived in one of the habitats?"

Sarah said with some surprise, "You saw those? You must have been in the elevator with the view, then."

Abraham continued. "We did, indeed, live in one of those for a time. It was exhilarating for a while, then merely interesting, but we missed the desert."

"What can you tell me of God's plan?" Caleb asked.

"I can tell you only in broad terms. I am not privy to your mission. So. Long ago, at the beginning, the garden was put here on this world for our God to live with his new creation, mankind. For a time, all was well. Then Lucifer, misunderstanding His intentions, believed mankind would be replacing the angels he'd given assignments to."

Abraham raised his finger to underscore his point. "Understand, Caleb, the angels had an important part in the preparation of this world. They helped prepare the garden and had much input into its design and beauty. The world back then was one large landmass. It was pure and pristine, livable, but not perfect like the garden. God wanted to make the entire world like the garden. That was part of mankind's purpose.

"So, Lucifer, thinking he was crafty, sought to twist the plan just enough to get God to abandon mankind and retain only his angels as his favorites. But our Lord loves us and would not. Down through the ages Lucifer continued to interfere, but even after all the times God's plan was hindered, He would not relent. Knowing the free will, He gave us was the weak link, He decided that to bring us back to Him He would need to do so personally.

"You know the rest. He, himself, paid the price to bring all the nations back to him, even those he'd given over to his council's authority."

Abraham put a hand on Caleb's shoulder. "The plan is to bring all creation back to him, not just mankind. That, I think, is where you and Anna enter the picture."

Puzzled more than ever, Caleb nodded and smiled. "Thank you for the explanation and for your hospitality."

"It is time for you to go," Abraham said, pointing into the sky where the globe approached from the desert.

"It has been an honor," Anna said, with wet eyes.

Sara hugged her and let her go as the globe silently came to rest a few inches from the sand.

Sandon and Lael, who'd found something else to do while Caleb and Anna visited, walked into view from around the corner of the house. They'd been in the orchards.

Lael handed Caleb a brown date he'd pulled from a tree. "The olives aren't ripe, but the dates are ready to pick."

They said their goodbyes and rode back to the elevator in silence.

The elevator continued up. Outside the window, the view was of distant stars and a clear view of massive habitats and ships under construction, all illuminated from above. Caleb, wondering where the light was coming from, turned to Lael, who pointed upward outside the window. Caleb looked up and saw that the tower expanded to hang suspended outward above them. White light shone from openings cut into the outer walls of the tower. He saw pulsing, swirling energies through massive clear glass windows.

Caleb nodded silently.

Caleb and Anna felt the elevator begin to slow and after a few minutes, it came to a stop with an end to the subsonic hum they'd stopped noticing after the first few minutes of their ascent. The door opened and Caleb felt a minute pressure change as his sinuses equalized. Anna put a hand to her nose and puffed.

A sign on the wall read, in blue letters, Level Six-Nine-Nine.

Following Lael and Sandon, they stepped out into a lobby.

Caleb's first thought was he'd walked into an airport lobby complete with reception desk and stewardesses walking about. A communications desk and wall panel sat in the middle of the room thirty feet away. Two women and a man were in deep discussion. One of the women turned at the sound of the elevator doors opening. Nudging the other woman, she smiled, walked forward, and bowed.

"Welcome, Commander Lael and Brother Sandon. This must be General Carson and Lady Hudson." She bowed to Caleb and Anna.

Caleb's brows rose.

Lael glanced at Caleb and smiled. "Didn't expect a promotion, did you? Don't concern yourself too much; you'll earn it."

Anna said to Sandon, "I'm a lady, now, am I?"

Sandon shrugged. "Of course. You've been called. That's part of it."

The receptionist said, "Step over here for a moment and we'll sign you in." She led them to the desk where a white disk rose from the desk and scanned each of them.

The man at the desk said, "You're early, it seems. Sometimes the council meetings run over." He got Lael's attention. "Sir, would you like us to take your charges to the commissary? There may be as much as a five hour wait."

"Of course. Good idea," Lael said and turned to Caleb. "You'll like the food and the atmosphere. I should take this time to check on a few things while you three relax."

The commissary was large enough to hold three or four hundred diners. A few other people were at tables eating and talking. Booths were set up at random throughout the space. Sandon led them to a booth near a window that showed a view of a great bay filled with shuttles and other craft. As they sat down, a screen popped up at the center of the table showing three dimensional views of various dishes.

"Wow, this all looks good," Anna said.

Sandon pointed to a pad on the table near his hand. "You put a finger here, like this, and think about the picture. The chef will show you pictures of dishes you desire most."

Anna did as he said and her screen changed to show a salad, with a plate of pasta and garlic bread. "This is exactly what I was thinking of. I'll have this."

Five seconds later a panel on the table slid aside and two plates rose up out of the table, hot and steamy.

"Ah, that was *really* fast," Anna said as Caleb did the same and a few seconds later a steamed fish with bread and roasted potatoes appeared before him.

Sandon ordered and they all tucked in. A few minutes later, with a mouth full of potatoes Caleb pointed at the craft sitting on the deck on the other side of the glass fifty feet away. "I'm not sure what to think about all those vehicles. The idea is still foreign to me. Isn't there a more spiritual, magical way angels and spirit beings get around? This looks a lot like science fiction."

Sandon nodded. "Our Lord God is all spirit. And some of his servants operate primarily outside of the physical, but they are the exception. There are no others like them. The rest of us are in a different sphere of reality. We are physical and will sometimes be given greater gifts as the need arises."

Anna said, "You mean it depends on your job?"

Sandon nodded. "That's right. If your mission requires it, you may travel by merely thinking about where you want to go."

"Like the warrior on the beach, I told you about?" Caleb asked.

"Exactly. And that gives you something to think about while I also run an errand." Sandon rose from his seat. "I'll be back in a few hours. Rest assured, we'll not be late to your meeting."

One end of the commissary held couches for relaxing after dinner, Anna assumed. She put her fork down. "I'm tired already. Let's go sit over there till Sandon comes back."

Caleb turned to see where she indicated. "Sure. We've got lots to discuss."

A few minutes later they were settled on a couch at the far end away from other diners. Anna sat next to Caleb, lay her head on his shoulder, and closed her eyes. He leaned back and studied the room. Almost nothing he had seen in the last few hours was like he had expected. Where were the angels floating around in white robes, with or without wings? The many craft were a bit of a shock. Especially the first ones he saw outside the tower. Their very existence raised so many questions. Had theologians gotten it so wrong?

Why had there been all the hyper-fantasy-like need to make heaven seem so foreign and unreachable? He suspected it had more to do with God's enemies desperately trying to make the afterlife seem unbelievable. Plus, to be honest, Caleb had seen a lot of this stuff in science fiction movies. He wondered if it was influenced by the angels who were kicked out of heaven. They, of course, would know exactly what heaven would be like—a lot like a science fiction movie. In the end, though, Caleb knew deep down in his heart this was what he really had wished for in moments back in the old life when he crouched in trenches, on cold nights and let himself think about it. After a few minutes, he closed his eyes and dreamed.

The weather was always nice in Paradise. Cool enough that a little exertion would leave you with only a thin sheen of perspiration which soon dried. And the air was clear enough that one could see almost all the way to the other side four hundred miles away where a wall of ice defined the boundary of this land. One large city sat in the middle of this great valley and many small villages dotted the land. Forests nested in scattered places interspersed with cultivated fields. No great river ran through it, but many small streams meandered unhurried through the fields and forests. Life was tranquil and there was plenty to do. Like the streams, no one was in a hurry.

When Caleb and his three men arrived and were let in the gate, it took them a few days to come to an acceptance of their new status. They were dead and this is where they would live till the great day of judgement came. Soon, his men found new friends and hobbies to occupy their time. Caleb saw little of them, which was okay because he met Anna Hudson.

No one in Paradise knew when judgement day would come, except for a few of the oldsters and they weren't talking. They would say, "Soon enough," insinuating when it came it would not be a pleasant experience. Of course, many of the ancients had already been here and gone, taken to a future at the perfect time to populate the new world and new heavenly city on the surface of the world.

Caleb and Anna connected so deeply and quickly it was almost scary. Within a few days of meeting for the first time, they were spending almost all their time together. They finished each other's sentences. They knew what the other preferred. They would sit for hours holding hands, saying nothing, then when they spoke it was in broad brushstrokes of understanding across a dense canvas of unspent emotion.

Time passed differently in Paradise. The wise men considered that time here happened quickly because no one had time to get bored.

A day came when Delphi, one of the guardian angels, approached. Caleb and Anna were at a stream, bare feet trailing in the water. Anna was teaching Caleb to weave a basket out of long grass. They chatted and smiled a lot as Caleb, with clumsy fingers, made a mess of his basket.

"Greetings, fellow pilgrims," Delphi said as he approached.

Caleb looked up. "Hello, Delphi. Want to learn how to make a basket?" Caleb held up his attempt at weaving the grass strands.

"Not if it's going to look like that." Delphi pointed a long finger at Anna's half-finished basket. "That one is coming along nicely, though."

Delphi sat down on the stream bank, his tall lanky form taking up as much space as Anna and Caleb did together. He sat quietly and watched the water dance across rocks.

Anna cocked her head, studying him, "What's on your mind, Delphi? I've never seen you unhappy."

"I bear sad news, Anna. Your time is at hand. I am to escort you to the gate. There, others will take you to be judged."

For a moment Anna was in shock. She put a hand over her mouth. The other hand went to hold Caleb's. After a moment she regained her composure and relaxed a little. "It's okay, Delphi, we've been good friends. I will miss you, but we'll see each other again."

Delphi nodded and raised himself from the grassy bank and stepped away to stand beneath a nearby tree and wait.

Caleb gripped both of Anna's hands. "Ahh, I don't know what to feel. I'm glad for you, but I'm afraid, too. It will be very difficult, I've heard so many times. I will miss you more than I've ever missed anything or anyone."

Anna pulled one hand free and lay it softly on Caleb's cheek. "Our Lord has brought us together. We will not long be apart."

Caleb raised his callused hand and covered hers. "You know I love you. I know you love me."

"I will say it anyway. Caleb, as sure as I live, I love you. Our Lord would not have brought us together to only tear us apart. As sure as we live, I know He will bring us back together."

Caleb, with wet eyes, kissed her lips and placed his forehead against hers. "So be it."

Caleb stood, raised her from the grass, and turned to Delphi who was watching them.

"Is it time?" Caleb asked.

Delphi waved them forward. "Yes, it is time. Let us go to the gate."

It took them three hours to walk to the gate. The fifty or so years Caleb had been there he'd not once climbed up the hill to the entrance where the fortress walls stood high and forbidding, the gate of tall, thick wood interspersed with hammered nails.

At the gate two angels waited in full armor, shields hanging from shoulders, long swords at the belt, and spears three times taller than a man in one hand pointing toward the sky.

One of them asked formally, "Anna Hudson, are you ready to appear before the throne?"

Anna, with her head high and shoulders back, said, "I am ready." She let go of Caleb's rough hand and stepped forward to judgement.

Three days later, they came for Caleb. He was not surprised. In fact, he was greatly pleased. He had spent the last three days wandering along the streets looking up old friends, reconnecting with the men who had been under his command.

A few hours later they walked out of the gate and standing outside the embattlement, the three of them disappeared in sparkles.

A moment later, Caleb, the two guards beside him, stood at the door of a great room. On either side tall, massive pillars marched away into the distance and as they did, seemed to shrink to half their size. At the far wall, a great chair sat at the center. On the chair sat the figure of a man, great and tall, white hair falling to his shoulders and encircled by a crown of gold. His eyes shone with starlight, full of arcane energies. Twenty-four lesser thrones sat on his right and twenty-four lesser thrones sat on his left. He was dressed in a white robe, purple sash at the waist.

Bright light filtered down from a great height, casting shadows among the pillars. Caleb shielded his eyes and saw a crowd of thousands seated on galleries on either side of a narrow aisle paved with grey marble. A short walk took them to a raised platform.

"Step up and stand before your judge," one of the angels said and pointed to the raised dais. As they all stepped onto the dais, it rose from the floor and glided down the aisle without a sound as the throne seemed to grow bigger. They stopped under a circle of whiter light and the two angels stepped back off the dais and stood at attention.

Another man stood beside the throne Caleb had not noticed at first. His stance was one of calm patience.

With a flash of light and smell of ozone a being, the likes Caleb had never seen before, appeared three steps down from the throne. He had the visage of a tailless lizard standing on two feet and his scales glistened. He descended the remaining four steps to the floor and his clawed feet tapped an unholy cadence.

He hissed, "I accuse you, Caleb Carson, of sin, gross and unholy, against your maker. You deserve death."

Caleb, glancing from one throne to the other, thought, This is not how I thought this would go.

"No," the accuser said, "You didn't. You have no secrets here. Even at this hour, you seek to escape the judgement you deserve. Your thoughts are clear to everyone in this room. Let us begin." The scaly accuser waved a claw. A large screen appeared hovering in the air.

"Do you see this? That is your mother. Why is she crying? You know. It is because you rebelled against her wishes and brought shame to your family. You lied to her and ran with untamed boys in your neighborhood. You stole and lied and lay violence against your neighbor."

"Wait a minute," Caleb blurted out, "I was only fourteen. I was young and, and stupid."

"Yes, you were, but this shows the kind of man you began as, and you never changed. You ended your life in violence on the battlefield, as we all know."

Caleb heard the words and knew the truth in them. He sputtered, but no words came.

The accuser continued. "We have many good examples from your life. You have been a very busy human. Notice this." The scene changed.

A battle ensued. Caleb stood behind a destroyed tank in full military gear, rifle in hand. A soldier shouted, shaking with fear. "We're getting slaughtered here sir, we need to retreat."

Caleb slapped the soldier across the face and shook him by the collar, "Get yourself together, soldier. Retreat is no option. Those bastards have got to die. Pick up your gun and follow me." Caleb released him and ran around the tank firing at any target he saw. The soldier followed and was immediately cut down, fell to the muddy ground, and lay still. Caleb turned to see the soldier fall. Without blinking an eye, he turned back to battle and pursued the enemy.

Face pale, Caleb stood stock still. He had forgotten that incident. It was one of many and one he wasn't proud of it. He should have retreated. He was a green lieutenant and he wanted revenge. He lost all but three of his men. He should have been canned, but the army needed killers and Caleb happened to be good at killing.

"Yes, you were a good killer. Do you know how much pain you caused over the years? How much suffering?" the accuser asked.

"But I learned my lesson. I tried to protect my men. I only killed people that needed killing." Caleb sputtered and trailed off.

"An old excuse for a dark-souled man who enjoys his profession."

Caleb stared at the screen in confusion. He thought, It's true. I did enjoy my profession, but not the killing--only the result.

The accuser stepped closer to Caleb and flashed a sharp-toothed smile. "Unfortunately, the result was almost always more killing."

For hours the scenes from his life unfolded. Finally, near the end, Caleb dropped to his knees and agreed. He deserved death.

For several minutes he knelt on the dais staring at the floor. He heard another voice and looked up. The accuser was nowhere to be seen. Rather, the man who stood beside the throne had voiced the words as he descended slowly down the step. He stopped and stood by the dais watching Caleb.

"Caleb Carson, observe," he said with a kind voice and waved a damaged hand in the air.

The screen changed to another scene. Caleb stood in swirling smoke, staring around at the battlefield around him. He was dirty, sweating, and breathing deeply. Blood was on his face and on the knife in his hand. An enemy lay at his feet. Many dead soldiers lay all around on the battlefield--friend and foe. The only two men from his unit to survive were the comm specialist and the chaplain. They stood behind him well outside striking range, watching him. The chaplain called, "Captain, you okay?"

Caleb turned at the sound of the chaplain's voice and dropped the knife. "Chaplain, why the hell, am I still alive? They're all dead." In a daze, he reached inside his gear and pulled out the small black bible the chaplain had given him a year before. He raised it. "I don't want this anymore."

The chaplin stepped closer and pointed to the bible. A bullet was lodged square in the middle. "Captain, I think you do."

Caleb stared at the bible, then around at the dead lying at his feet. Exhausted in body and spirit, he dropped to his knees. "Chaplain, please. Tell me what to do."

The man with the damaged hand turned to God on the throne and said, "That day he became one of mine. He is one of the redeemed." He turned to Caleb and stretched out his hand. "Rise, brother."

The figure on the center throne rose to his feet. The air hazed with sparkles of stars. Crackling streamers of energy rose from the throne and thunder rumbled around the great hall. The forty-eight elders rose from their thrones and all others in the colossal room stood.

With a deep bass cry, His voice echoing off the chamber's far wall, God spoke: "This man is forgiven. He is mine." He sat back down. All went dark.

Caleb opened his eyes to find Anna staring intently into them. She asked, "Did you have a memory? There are tears in your eyes." Caleb put his arms around her and whispered, "God is good!"

CHAPTER TWENTY-TWO

When Sandon and Lael returned, Caleb and Anna were still sitting on the couches in the commissary. When Sandon saw their demeanor, he said, "Something has changed."

Anna looked up from the couch. "Fifteen years ago, I remembered standing before our Lord under judgement. Caleb remembered his trial only half an hour ago."

"I see." Sandon spread his hands. "It will take time to come to terms with those memories."

"Not a problem," Caleb said, standing up from the couch. "He forgave me. That's enough understanding for now. I'm ready to get to it."

Lael smiled. "Just the man for the job, brother." He slapped Caleb on the shoulder.

Caleb staggered. "Easy, Commander. I'm only human."

"True, but not just any human. Let's go." He pointed to the shield and sword wrapped in bedding Caleb had been carrying everywhere with them. "Grab your gear."

They left the commissary and went back to the front desk and com center there.

"Our appointment still good?" Lael asked the attendant.

She put a hand on the pad. "There is a change. You and Brother Sandon are to accompany the called to the Star Room."

Lael's brow rose. "The Star Room, nice. It's been a while." Lael turned to the others. "This will be a treat. You'll see what I mean."

They walked deeper into the tower, past another set of windows showing the hanger where the many craft sat. They turned down a hall and came to double doors, which slid open at their approach.

Lael said, "This elevator will take us up to the, what do you call it, ah, 'officer country.'"

Riding up the elevator, Caleb held Anna's hand. He asked Lael, "Am I supposed to salute or anything?"

"Just a shallow bow or a nod. Relax, follow my lead. It will go well. You'll see."

The elevator came to a stop. The doors opened to reveal a lobby. A woman in a plain white uniform approached. "Our Lord is expecting you." She indicated the gear Caleb carried. "You can leave that by the door. Come this way." She turned and walked across the room. Two angels in exquisite livery stood at attention, smiled at their approach, quietly took Caleb's wrapped weapons, and opened the doors inward into a dark room.

"This is the Star Room." She led them into the room, waving toward the steps to a platform a few feet higher. A dim light shone down onto the center of the platform where Jesus stood quietly waiting.

When they stepped up, Jesus smiled and stepped forward. He shook hands with Lael, then pulled him into a casual hug and let go, patting him on the back. He turned to Sandon, gave him a casual hug also.

When he came to Anna, she raised clasped hands and dropped to her knees. "My Lord. I am...overcome."

Jesus took her hands. "Anna, all is well. Stand." He helped her to her feet. "I see you are well and in good company," he said, glancing at Caleb with a smile.

Caleb nodded. "My Lord," he said, feeling like dropping to his knees, also.

Jesus smiled and shook Caleb's hand firmly. "I'm glad you chose to come. I've been looking forward to speaking with you since the last time we met."

"My Lord, I remembered that meeting not an hour ago. I must say, 'thank you.'"

Jesus looked him in the eyes "You're welcome, Caleb. There is a reason I wanted it fresh in your mind. There is much I wish to discuss, much I want you to see."

Jesus turned and waved his hand around the dark room. "This is our star room. It is here to remind us of our purpose and our hope. Sometimes men, and even spirits, speak so glibly of the universe and their place in it. They seek to understand the infinite and fail. Only our Father God understands that. He embodies it in Himself. He has placed it in our hands to be His imagers to the universe."

Jesus turned back to them. "Anna, what do you think of the tower and our budding city?"

Anna almost rolled her eyes, trying to think of an adequate answer.

"Relax, Anna. You will not be graded," Jesus laughed heartily. "I like to get feedback. The city descended only three hundred years ago. It will continue to grow for ten-thousand years and more. Right now, it feels almost hollow. Only a few have arrived so far. Eventually, all will be here, and this city will be a bustling metropolis, the greatest city among a million cities and the home of God; an example to the rest of the world and to the stars."

He turned to Caleb. "I know you have questions about *that*."

"Ah, yes uh, Sire. About the city. I remember hearing a sermon once, that the saved go to heaven immediately after death, also the part about the stars. I've wondered about that, too."

"Good, you've had plenty of time to ponder the subject. Do you know how long you were in Paradise waiting for judgement?"

"About fifty years?"

"Thirteen hundred and twelve years. Didn't seem like it, though, did it? Concerning the stars: you see, our Father loves all his creation and wishes every living being to share in his perfect society. He wishes every living thing to reflect his image."

"Are you saying there are people out there among the stars?"

Jesus nodded. "Not quite like you, but yes, in the way that matters. Even a few of the stars, themselves."

"And by reflecting his image you mean…?"

"I mean all sentient life will love the way our Father loves and all the rest of creation will support that."

"I hear what you say, and it sounds great to me, but I admit I just can't picture it," Caleb said, shaking his head.

"That's okay. You don't need to picture it you'll get the chance to see it."

Jesus turned to Lael. "Commander, are your preparations in place?"

Lael nodded. "Yes, Lord."

"Good, you'll be leaving in seven days. Have your men take time off to pray and prepare themselves."

"Yes, Lord."

"Take Sandon with you and show him around. He has a part in this."

"Yes, Lord." Lael motioned to Sandon, and they left the star room, leaving Jesus alone with Caleb and Anna.

Jesus said, "You may be wondering why I called you both. Caleb, you recall I was present at your judgement. I witnessed your life. I was impressed by your tenacious nature. But more importantly, I know your heart. I know you did what you could to relieve suffering. It, also, is a strong part of your character. The same goes for you, Anna, and is one reason why I arranged for you to be with each other in Paradise. It is also why your love for the other is so strong."

Anna took Caleb's hand.

Jesus turned around and walked a few feet away gesturing in the air. As he turned back, the room began to brighten. Stars flared on and slowly spun around in the air around them. After a few seconds, the room was fully illuminated by a myriad of stars.

Jesus said, "This is creation. All these lights in space have the necessary ingredients for life. These stars have intelligence so far." As he said the words, sixteen stars flared into bright green. "Of these stars, three are having problems.

And this one," a star flared red, "I am sending Lael and Sandon with a cohort of two thousand of my holy guard to correct that problem. And I'm asking if you and Anna will be willing to go with him and help in whatever way you can."

Caleb, mind in turmoil, said, "Lord, I am willing, but I'm just a simple soldier. I saw the way one of your angels fought. He's way more able than I will ever be."

Jesus touched the red star as it slowly spun past, A screen high and wide blazed into view showing a scene of devastation. Giant machines dug into the ground ripping up great swaths of earth. People, tall, thin, and bluish in color trudged across a barren land of swirling dust and smoke, carrying burdens, obviously starving. Iron collars were around their necks and cables chained them together. Sitting astride nightmarish creatures, grey bat-winged slavers prodded them with long poles.

"Observe, General Carson and Lady Hudson. I have fifty thousand infantry who have been training for five years. They are yours to command. Take them with you. I wish for you to deliver a message for me."

Jesus looked them both over carefully, then with fire in his eyes, he said, "My message is simple: 'Let my people go.'"

After gathering his gear, Caleb and Anna left the upper levels and met Lael and Sandon at the commissary. They were standing by the windows watching the sleek craft land and take off.

"We're ready to leave when you guys are," Caleb said as they came to a stop by the windows.

"Good." Lael pointed to the sight outside the window. The great bay held many transports from one-man globes to hardened craft of a military nature ranging from two-man scouts up to three long and narrow transports capable of carrying thousands of men and equipment. "I'm thinking we should take one of those, so I can show you both around a little."

"Sounds great, let's do it," Caleb said and hefted the wrapped blade and shield. "I'd like to return this, soon. It's heavy."

"We'll find out where Centurion Elazar is and arrange to meet. Meanwhile, let's get to our shuttle and go meet your officers."

Caleb's pulse quickened at the mention of the infantry. He didn't miss the mention of Elazar's unexpected rank but took it in stride. He felt deeply out of his depth and excited at the same time. He and Anna followed Lael and Sandon out of the commissary and to an elevator that took them two floors down and opened into the cavernous bay. Parked on the deck nearby, within easy walking distance, sat a sleek craft of seeming white porcelain with stubby wings and large clear windows.

Two men and a woman stood at attention by the ramp and saluted with an open right hand over the heart. They all were dressed in a simple light grey one piece uniform with a starburst on the right chest. Their hair was cut short, except for the woman whose hair was cropped just below ear level.

The woman stepped forward as they approached. "Commander and Brother." She nodded to Lael and Sandon, then turned to Caleb. General and Lady, this way, please."

One of the crewmembers stepped forward and took the wrapped parcel from Caleb and carried it into the craft.

"I'm Sub-captain, Valentina. I will be your pilot." She entered the craft and went forward while the other crew showed them to their seats.

They sat, the craft rose smoothly, and turned to the huge doors at one end of the great room.

A smaller opening appeared in the wall, and they exited into a night filled with sparkling lights dimmed only by rays shining down from the huge portholes in the globe sitting atop the tower. The Milky Way seemed to turn sharply as they angled toward the tower and descended.

"I thought you might want to see the tower from the outside," Valentina said. They descended slowly on antigravity, and, after a few minutes, the frigid cold of the atmosphere created patterns of frozen moisture on the forward screens and the viewports to be later melted by the craft's internal heating systems.

The world below seemed to grow larger, snow-covered mountains rising above the clouds giving way to the scattered greens and tan and gray of the surface still many miles away below them.

The pilot stayed within a few miles of the tower, keeping it to the starboard so Caleb and Anna had an uninterrupted view. As they descended, they encountered many craft entering and exiting hatches on the side of the tower like honeybees swarming a hive.

Valentina said, "I know the tower appears the same width as near the ground, but it is only twenty miles on a side up here, not the fifty miles at ground level."

Caleb noticed below them that five craft hovered close to the tower and touched it. "What are those five craft doing down there?"

"Good that you noticed," the pilot said. "They're unloading supplies. Those are the levels six hundred to six twenty. That's our destination. It's where you'll meet your troops."

Caleb glanced to Lael who stood beside him, "I'd like to get word to my friends in the garden. I think they will want to see this."

Lael nodded. "Of course. I suppose you'd like to give them a position as specialists under your command."

"Yeah, I think they would like that."

A few minutes later the pilot swung the craft toward the tower and descended directly to a hatch that opened as they grew close. They entered into a white corridor and, after a few seconds slowly floated into a chamber where five other small craft sat on a polished metal floor.

As Valentina brought the craft to the deck, she said, "I hope you enjoyed the tour, General and Lady. It has been my pleasure." She grounded the craft and touched controls. The door opened and they exited.

CHAPTER TWENTY-THREE

The day on the beach was warm as usual, but Abdul didn't mind. The cool breeze blew through the flimsy walls of the shack he'd found on the beach and the shade kept the sun off his face. As usual, he woke from his daytime sleep as the sun was going down. He felt distracted and disturbed. He'd had a dream about fishing, and it had not gone well. Sitting up on the straw pallet he'd laid a blanket over, he rubbed his face and glanced out toward the familiar water. He stopped rubbing his face and stared; a man was out there sitting on the sand by his boat, his face toward the waves.

Cautious, Abdul rose, took a long drink from a jug by the doorway, and stepped out. He looked around, up and down the beach, and saw no one else, then walked slowly toward the stranger.

"Ho, stranger," he called.

Jesus, still sitting, turned, and looked him up and down. "Do you own this boat?"

Abdul stopped. "I think so. No one else is using it."

Jesus stood and wiped sand from his legs. "I want to catch a few fish. Can you take me out?"

"Oh, no. I fish alone."

Jesus said, "I see," and turned to face to waves.

Abdul stepped closer and put a hand on the rim of the boat. He pointed up the beach. "There are many close to town who would be happy to take you out on the water."

Jesus turned back to him. "But the best fishing is right here," he said placing a flat palm on the sand.

"Yes, the fishing is good." Abdul watched the stranger, looking for the subtle clues that told him the real story of a man's character.

Jesus nodded and turned to the boat. A small net lay over the side where it had dried in the heat of the day. "Did you make this net? It seems to be made quite well."

"I, ah, yes, from the long grass nearby. Are you a fisherman?"

"There was a time I fished a lot. I caught much fish of all kinds," Jesus said.

"I stay out all night and only come back after the sun has come back up. Most people would only fish for a few hours. So, you see, I must go alone."

Jesus produced a bag Abdul had not noticed before. "I have enough food and water for the whole night. See," Jesus opened the bag and pulled out a water bottle, exactly like the kind Abdul's father had made by hand and showed him the fish cooked in seaweed like Abdul's mother did long ago. Abdul could smell it from ten feet away.

"I…I like it quiet and…I don't like the boat to rock too much… and I fix my own bait," Abdul stuttered.

"Okay, I can be quiet and still. Maybe we'll catch a few good ones, heh?" Jesus put a hand on the boat. "Let's get her in the water, but first, I'll wait here for you to get your provisions."

Abdul stood in troubled confusion for a few seconds, then turned to the shack and came back a few seconds later with a wooden bucket in one hand containing fish parts and a small bag in the other.

Minutes later, they were out on the open water, heading still further out, Abdul silent at the rudder.

Abdul knew these waters well. Not only did he have a sense of where the fish would be, but he also could sense the ebb and flow of life underwater, much like a good stockbroker sensed the flow of wealth, when to lower the bait and when to pull it all in.

After an hour of rowing, in which Jesus helped, they came near to the spot Abdul liked best.

Abdul stood in the boat and looked out onto the dark water, moonlight reflecting off shallow waves, then he sat back down and glanced up to the stars.

Jesus took the paddle in hand, turned to Abdul, and pointed thirty degrees away from the land.

Abdul frowned, thinking to go that way, then with a growing, grudging respect, nodded.

A few minutes later, they let the boat coast to a stop and bob in the water as Abdul threw a little bait on the water to attract whatever fish were near the surface.

As the night wore on, Jesus anticipated Abdul's intentions and helped.

The fishing went well. They caught a few of Abdul's favorites and of a good size. Abdul held up a fish by the gills and spoke the first words in three hours. "I caught one of these last night—I call them redfins—twice this long. They're good eating and sell fast at the market."

Jesus nodded and smiled, admiring the fish and the fisherman. A few minutes later, he pointed to a star. "What is that star's name?"

Abdul looked up. "Oh, that's Panya. Next to it is Anippe, then over there is Amun and Sara."

Jesus nodded and smiled and waited patiently.

"It does get lonely out here sometimes. The stars are my friends," Abdul said, a few minutes later.

Soon, they pulled another big one in. Abdul smiled broadly. "This is only the second time I've caught one of these. I'll keep this one and smoke it for myself."

Jesus asked, "What is it called?"

Abdul shrugged. "I don't know. I've only fished these waters a few years."

"What do you mean? You didn't grow up around here?"

"Ah, no. I mean, I woke up nearby a few years ago and found this boat and started fishing. I wandered where I was for a while. I decided not to think too hard about that."

They were silent for another hour.

Abdul broke the silence. "Where did you learn to read the water so well?"

Jesus laughed. "All over. I've fished in every ocean, in every river."

"You fish well," Abdul said. He had been putting bait to a hook. He stopped and looked up. "But you don't seem to be a fisherman. Did you have your own boat? When did you have time to fish in all those places?"

"Good question, Abdul. Where did you grow up, what country?"

Abdul finished placing the bait and threw the line over the side. He paused a moment to dredge up the old memory from deep down. "Crete. I was raised in Crete."

After those words, they stayed silent till the sun rose and the stars merged with the sky.

They headed back to shore with the current Abdul knew well.

In silence, Jesus helped Abdul pull the boat onto the sand and take the many fish over to the shack.

On the outside of the shack, a board had been placed on pegs set into the wall where fish could be placed high enough that roaming animals could not reach. Abdul dumped the last bucket on the board and turned to Jesus.

"Tell me where you're from. Why are you here?"

Jesus looked up at the glow from high above, "See that light? I live up there."

"What?"

"Listen, Abdul. When the Spartan pirates raided your village and took your father and mother and brothers away, I understood your pain and loneliness. They are all here and I know where you can find them."

Jesus placed a hand on Abdul's shoulder, then stepped back. And to be sure of the right impression, he vanished in a blinding flash and clap of thunder, leaving a hole in the sand a foot deep. Abdul lay where he'd fallen ten feet away and watched sand and sizzling stars fall to the ground.

The next morning at dawn, Abdul left his boat behind, and with hope and a grim determination, headed for the tower.

CHAPTER TWENTY-FOUR

The current was not swift; it was easy to paddle up the stream toward the old city. After a few miles, Jake, Chen, and Boris brought the boat to the bank, tied it off, and headed up the valley. A half-mile from the old city, they saw the remains of the fourth temple, the one built after Satan's first defeat. It had served nearly a thousand years but was no longer needed. A few broken pillars still stood, moss covered, higher than the treetops.

On the outskirts, a hamlet of small homes had been built from stone and whatever else was at hand. They passed others going in both directions.

A street came into view; all was in ruins. There was very little sign of the technologically advanced city of Jerusalem that existed in the twenty-first century. The city was damaged severely in the last great war and never rebuilt. There was no longer a need for the city either; all that remained was the rubble of the old city and the temple in its midst, forever a testament to the life and ministry of the savior.

The three men stood on the street where stones and wood had been moved to make a path. "Not exactly what I expected," Jake said.

Boris picked up a stone by his feet and tossed it on top of a pile. "Yeah, I'd heard that no one lived in the old city. Now I know why."

When the men returned to the great tree, they found their friends in deep conversation with the great prophet Isaiah who was sitting on a bench. They were all listening to Oscar explaining what he'd learned as a kid in Scotland.

Isaiah said, "Oscar, my son, you wouldn't believe all the strange sayings I've heard from people who lived after my time. The farther removed in time, the more strange they became."

Helen said, "I know what you mean. In my first life, a preacher came to my village and started telling everyone God created hell, then created everyone for hell to suffer forever. It was like he knew nothing of God's love or His plan."

As he approached, Chen heard what they were talking about. He interrupted, "It makes the Lord sound like Satan." They all turned to him.

Isaiah said, "Yes, it is an attack used to drive believers from the Way. Many have turned from our Lord thinking he cared not for them nor most of creation."

Chen turned to Isaiah and bowed deeply. "Pardon my intrusion, Prophet. I did not mean to interrupt."

"No harm done. We all here now have sure knowledge of the Way and our future."

Daniel, kneeling on the grass, asked, "What was it like at the old city?"

"All in ruins, so we came back," Jake said.

Isaiah rose from the bench. "It has been my honor to speak with you." He bowed. They thanked him and watched him walk away to disappear down one of the paths.

"Great, huh?" Oscar turned to the others. "I still have a lot of questions, but I feel better, now."

"So, what do we do now?" Jake said. "We can get back on the boat and visit the other shrines. Maybe find a library or something."

As Jake spoke, they felt a stirring in the wind. Fruit pods hanging nearby began swaying in slow circles. The air became charged, and sparkles filled the air. With a soft pop, the stars faded, and Caleb, Lael, Anna, and Sandon appeared, standing on the moss covered ground under the tree thirty feet away.

Caleb blinked and looked around, then with a smile, held his hands out wide and said, "Look who appeared out of thin air."

Helen, sitting on the grass, stood. "Where did you guys come from?"

They all crowded around.

"How did it go?" Beatrice asked.

Anna said, "It went well. We met Abraham and Sarah—yeah, *that* Abraham and Sarah. Then we met with Jesus, and He gave us a mission. You will hardly believe it; I hardly believe it myself."

Jake said, "Okay, I want to hear about this mission."

Smiling, Caleb slapped Jake on the shoulder. "Sure. We can all talk on the elevator."

The ride up the elevator was fun as Caleb and Anna stood back from the window and watched their friends exclaim in wonder.

While they rose higher and the view outside the window expanded, Caleb asked Lael, "What's the itinerary, now?"

"We're leaving in seven days. The troops are on leave, but now, it's time to meet the men under your direct command. Then we have a council of war."

Something had puzzled Anna the last few hours. Since getting in the elevator, it had formed into a question.

Sandon saw Anna's frown. He asked, "Anna, what's on your mind? You seem perplexed."

"I am." Anna spread her hands out, indicating the elevator and the view outside. "What is so special about all of us that we get to ride all the way to the top while most of humanity is required to climb through all the levels? Why did we get to skip all that?"

Sandon smiled. "I've been waiting for you to get to that question." He glanced around at the others. "It is simple. You all, here, are ready enough to be used for a greater purpose. It doesn't mean you've arrived at spiritual perfection. Some day you will want to visit all the different levels and discover the lessons to be learned there. Even members of the heavenly host need reminding, occasionally.

"The words of the apostles are appropriate; Paul, who has ridden this elevator, said, 'And we know all things work together for good to them who love God, to them who are the called according to his purpose.' All of you, here, have been called—you and Caleb, Jake, Chen, and Boris, to go to the stars and rescue those enslaved. The others are to help in other ways. Our God has seen the love in your hearts and deemed you worthy of this calling--this adventure for you. Just because he called you doesn't mean a few others are not qualified, but it was you he called for this specific purpose.

"Paul also said, 'For whom he did foreknow, he preordained that they would be conformed to the image of his son.' There's more, as you know, but the point is some are ready for greater purpose when they arrive in heaven and others need much time and growth to be useful for anything greater than continuing life as before, however much better it is here.

"Sadly, for most people, life will continue as before. The lessons they didn't learn, then, will need to be learned, eventually. The tower and the Lord's presence is a constant reminder, till they are ready to take the journey and enter in."

Sandon paused. "Does that answer your question?"

Anna heard the words and couldn't help but lower her eyes in humility. She said, "Yes. I've wondered about many things. You've answered more than one question. Thank you."

Sandon placed a hand on Anna's shoulder. "You're welcome, my friend."

Helen, Oscar, Beatrice, and Daniel stood at the port window staring outward into space. A few miles away, four craft, each a mile long, sat stolid and powerful, white, and gleaming. The last of the supplies and equipment had been loaded and the shuttle their friends, Caleb, Anna, and the others were in, was entering the cavern-like mouth of the lead ship. Soon they would be on their way.

"Do you wish you were going?" Helen asked Oscar.

"Ah, no way. I'll stay here. I've got too many questions."

"Are you going back to the university?" Helen asked, grinning.

"No. Why memorize books when I can talk with the people who were there. I'm starting in the garden, then I'm going to start climbing. I have all the time I need. It will be wonderful."

Helen put an arm around Oscar and hugged him. "Mind if I join you?"

"Not at all. It will be great."

"Us, too."

Helen turned to Daniel and Beatrice. "All the merrier."

Oscar smiled as he thought of the adventure ahead. "We can..."

As they discussed the plans for their upcoming adventure, the craft outside the window flared and winked out leaving only stars.

Chapter Twenty-Five

Elder stood before the canvas and studied it. Something was still missing, even after all the hours, he'd put into it. But he knew he was close and sought for a last surge of inspiration. He stepped back a few feet to get a better overall view and saw, not a city in progress--a tower surrounded by large swaths of open space interspersed with smaller cities and towns—but a finished city, magnificent and encompassing, dominating the skyline as far as one could see.

He saw a city of glass spires and gold arches, of white marble buildings, stretching up and out, hugging the tower, rising even up through the clouds. People buzzed around the city in fantastic vehicles. Ships cruised the waters silenty.

On the horizon, the sun arrived on its morning course, unneeded in this part of the world, for, from above, white light bathed the city in streamers through the clouds—gleaming, revealing fingers touching the city, leaving speckles of light.

Elder had done as Captain Newton suggested. He visited the city and it had not taken him long to understand that the soul of this city was the soul of its architect. He stood before the canvas, brush in hand, and prayed.

The tower rose high above the world, a shining candle--a beacon to the universe.

Inside the top level, Jehovah watched from above the pillar of swirling plasma, which cast shadows among the Cherubim. At the foot of the throne, on the golden floor beneath, Jesus knelt in prayer.

The Lord God felt the universe around him and approved.

He shifted His attention to the world beneath. He saw Eden city nestled at the entrance to the tower and knew the yearning of the souls living there. He heard their prayers and heeded. He saw New Jerusalem's encompassing walls and its twelve gates and knew every soul who passed through.

He knew every frailty, every desire, and the determination of every soul on the earth below.

He focused upon the cottage at the edge of the river and the artist inside. Elder stood at the canvas with an easel in hand mixing white with a bit of gold. He made the last brushstroke. As a tear of satisfaction tracked down his cheek, the brush fell from his hand.

God above pulsed with the frequency of love. Observing all He had made, He spoke, and all creation felt His voice, "It is good."

The paddle wheel on the riverboat churned and splashed the old familiar rhythm. Captain Newton sat forward on the top deck, a glass of iced tea in hand watching the southern tip of Africa pass by. The first mate was at the wheel. He was on another trip around the world and excited to discover what new things had happened in the last two hundred fifty years since his last great journey. A wave of contentment passed through him causing his arms and legs to tingle and knew then that God had just now spoken and was pleased with the world. Smiling, he wondered what new things he would see this time as he sipped, then began singing with a pleasant baritone, "Amazing grace, how sweet the sound, that saved a wretch like me…"

In Brazil, on a high plateau, sat a monastery nestled among craggy rocks and knarly trees. Juan San Marco de Guez, formerly a priest, sat cross-legged with scissors in one hand and clippings of his long black beard in his lap. He stared in the direction of Jerusalem for a moment, then raising the scissors, continued removing his beard, his promise to God abandoned, forgiveness accepted.

Lilly Primrose was on her knees pulling weeds when she saw the stranger coming down the path from Mr. Gallagher's house. But it wasn't her neighbor, this time. She'd had a difficult few weeks since she'd fallen in the stream. Many memories had returned, and her days were often filled with a vague unease. Nervously, she rose from her knees and wiped her hands on the apron tied around her waist.

As the stranger approached, she saw him carrying a package in white cloth. It wasn't till he stopped a few feet away she saw he had a little dog in his arms. She stepped closer and he held out to her a little white chihuahua with a clipped ear. She looked the stranger in the eyes and saw that he wasn't a stranger. As she held her little-long lost friend in her arms, she stepped closer and laid her head against his chest.

Jesus said, "All is well, Lilly," as he put his arms around her and held her tight.

In Savannah, Georgia, Maria Rosetta Garcia, stepped carefully, a month old infant cradled in her arms. From the path, she could see the birthing shrine clearly. The door was closed, indicating a new soul had arrived. She smiled happily and proceeded up the path, careful not to stub her toe.

On the world beneath, sleepers awoke, and workers lifted their hands from their labors. They heard their God and worshipped.

...and then...

CPSIA information can be obtained
at www.ICGtesting.com
Printed in the USA
BVHW071501310522
638504BV00008B/45